NEW DIRECTIONS FOR COMMUNITY COLL

Arthur M. Cohen
EDITOR-IN-CHIEF

Florence B. Brawer
ASSOCIATE EDITOR

Pam Schuetz
PUBLICATION COORDINATOR

Help Wanted: Preparing Community College Leaders in a New Century

William E. Piland
San Diego State University

David B. Wolf
Western Association of Colleges and Schools

EDITORS

Number 123, Fall 2003

JOSSEY-BASS
San Francisco

HELP WANTED: PREPARING COMMUNITY COLLEGE LEADERS IN A NEW CENTURY
William E. Piland, David B. Wolf (eds.)
New Directions for Community Colleges, no. 123

Arthur M. Cohen, Editor-in-Chief
Florence B. Brawer, Associate Editor

Copyright © 2003 Wiley Periodicals, Inc., A Wiley Company. All rights reserved. No part of this publication may be reproduced, stored in a retrieval system, or transmitted in any form or by any means, electronic, mechanical, photocopying, recording, scanning, or otherwise, except as permitted under Sections 107 or 108 of the 1976 United States Copyright Act, without either the prior written permission of the Publisher or authorization through payment of the appropriate per-copy fee to the Copyright Clearance Center, 222 Rosewood Drive, Danvers, MA 01923, (978) 750-8400, fax (978) 750-4744. Requests to the Publisher for permission should be addressed to the Permissions Department, c/o John Wiley & Sons, Inc., 111 River St., Hoboken, NJ 07030; (201) 748-8789, fax (201) 748-6326, e-mail: permreq@wiley.com

New Directions for Community Colleges is indexed in Current Index to Journals in Education (ERIC).

Microfilm copies of issues and articles are available in 16mm and 35mm, as well as microfiche in 105mm, through University Microfilms Inc., 300 North Zeeb Road, Ann Arbor, Michigan 48106-1346.

ISSN 0194-3081   electronic ISSN 1536-0733

NEW DIRECTIONS FOR COMMUNITY COLLEGES is part of The Jossey-Bass Higher and Adult Education Series and is published quarterly by Wiley Subscription Services, Inc., A Wiley Company, at Jossey-Bass, 989 Market Street, San Francisco, California 94103-1741. Periodicals postage paid at San Francisco, California, and at additional mailing offices. POSTMASTER: Send address changes to New Directions for Community Colleges, Jossey-Bass, 989 Market Street, San Francisco, California 94103-1741.

SUBSCRIPTIONS cost $70.00 for individuals and $149.00 for institutions, agencies, and libraries. Prices subject to change.

EDITORIAL CORRESPONDENCE should be sent to the Editor-in-Chief, Arthur M. Cohen, at the ERIC Clearinghouse for Community Colleges, University of California, 3051 Moore Hall, Box 951521, Los Angeles, California 90095-1521. All manuscripts receive anonymous reviews by external referees.

Cover photograph © Rene Sheret, After Image, Los Angeles, California, 1990.

CONTENTS

EDITORS' NOTES

The two of us have spent most of our adult lives in and around community colleges. Over this time, we have been a part of the evolution of the community college as it has grown and responded, taking its place now as a powerful force for the advancement of American society. We are persuaded that community colleges are a vital and permanent, if underappreciated, part of higher education in our country.

We are equally persuaded that community colleges, like any other type of complex organization, must have competent leadership to be effective. We have come to understand that leadership in higher education is distributed: it is exercised by members of the faculty, by key members of the support staff, and certainly by administrators and members of governing boards. (We note as well the importance of student leadership; however, we leave to other, more qualified, writers the task of discussing student leadership development issues.)

As we begin the twenty-first century, we note that community college leadership has never been more complex and challenging. The distributed nature of leadership is inherently complicated. Add to this the intricacies of serving new populations and local needs, state law and coordinating agencies, state and local budgeting systems, unstable financial environments, collective bargaining, capital construction bonding, federal labor law, instructional and administrative technology, calls for accountability including the assessment of learning, articulation with high schools and baccalaureate institutions—phew! There is a lot to understand.

We have had the opportunity to work with a large number of colleges—and college leaders—for an extended number of years. Even as the community college has exhibited its importance as never before, we must also observe that the current state of community college leadership is not good. Indeed, we would join with those who have labeled the current situation a "crisis." The evidence of this circumstance can be found in the reluctance of faculty to assume faculty leadership roles; the limited number of faculty members and others who move into junior administrative roles; the increasing tendency to seek leadership talent from outside the academy in some areas of specialty (for example, personnel, finance, information technology); the reduction in the size (and quality) of candidate pools drawn to middle management and senior executive positions; the difficulty frequently experienced in drawing women and persons of color into these pools; the limited access most leaders and could-be leaders have to high-quality, sustained opportunities for development; and the typically poor sets of support systems and local institutional incentives and policies that would encourage leadership development.

New Directions for Community Colleges, no. 123, Fall 2003   © Wiley Periodicals, Inc.

We have been increasingly concerned about this state of affairs and, for the past several years, have been working with others to better understand the problem and develop responses to it. That is what this volume is about. We are joined in this project by an accomplished set of scholars and practitioners similarly concerned about community college leadership and its development.

James G. March, professor emeritus at Stanford University and one of the most respected thinkers about organizational phenomena, and Stephen S. Weiner, a distinguished higher education leader and former member of the Board of Governors of the California Community Colleges, set the stage. They discuss the nature of leadership in higher education generally and community colleges in particular. They not only note the dynamism and complexity of leading in the twenty-first century but further illuminate changes in the community college environment that make for extraordinary claims on leaders. Central to their concerns is the notion of civility, and they propose some simple steps to advance it.

George Boggs, president of the American Association of Community Colleges, then uses information collected by his organization and others to provide a national perspective. He articulates a concern for the flow of leaders based on expansion of the demand for community college services just as a wave of retirements in the corps of leaders will surge. The development of leaders is advanced by an exposition of the skills that contemporary leaders must master and the policies that colleges might foster to encourage this activity.

Joanne Cooper, professor of education at the University of Hawaii, Manoa, and president of the university's academic senate, and Louise Pagotto, assistant dean of arts and sciences at Kapiʻolani Community College, remind us of the importance of faculty leadership and that almost all who move into administrative roles came from the faculty ranks. The authors have initiated and are deeply involved with the implementation of an innovative faculty leadership development program. They discuss its features and its performance.

Chris McCarthy, recently appointed president of Napa Valley College, reflects on the roles of faculty and administrative leader and the peculiarities of making the transition from one to the other. As one who has made his way up this classic path, the author shares important observations, emphasizing with appropriate humor the interpersonal dimensions of the journey. He also provides a most insightful list of personal attributes that would benefit anyone moving into middle management.

George B. Vaughan, long-time community college leader and now scholar at North Carolina State University at Raleigh, and Iris M. Weisman, associate professor of higher education at Antioch University McGregor in Yellow Springs, Ohio, focus on the preparation of community college presidents. Noting the unique features of the presidency and the increasing problems evident in securing appropriate candidates for this role, they urge individual college campuses to accept the responsibility for preparing future presidents. They call on boards of trustees and presidents to design, recruit for, and carry out community college-based programs and provide details on how this might be done.

Betty Duvall, professor of higher education and coordinator of the community college leadership program at Oregon State University in Corvallis, describes university-based community college leadership programs. She confirms the centrality of Ed.D. and Ph.D. programs and provides information about national availability. Changes to these programs that would make them more appropriate for aspiring leaders in the twenty-first century are discussed. Most significantly, Duvall identifies the limitations of the university as a provider of leadership development services for aspiring community college leaders.

Cristina Chiriboga, currently vice president of instruction at Cuyamaca College in El Cajon, California, and completing her doctoral studies, provides a careful examination of a leadership development program offered by a statewide professional association. Data gathered from both presenters and participants in the program were analyzed to arrive at a profile of its strengths and weaknesses. Case studies of this sort are few in number and sorely needed.

Constance M. Carroll, president of San Diego Mesa College and long prominent in the area of leadership development, and Martha G. Romero, professor of higher education at Claremont Graduate University in California and director of its Community College Leadership Development Initiatives, review the origins, design, and implementation of the program. This different approach to leadership development weds an ambitious range of intentions with a large and various group of providers. The early successes of this effort suggest a new, more diversified, regionally oriented basis for serving emerging and established leaders.

Drawing on the work of all of our colleagues, the two of us share our concerns and ideas. We believe that the challenge of providing development programming for community college leaders is among the two or three most important issues facing the enterprise. To overcome this crisis will require departures from the patterns with which we have grown comfortable, new thinking, and sustained effort. But meeting the challenge provides the promise of well-prepared and motivated leaders for community colleges far into the new century. Concluding this volume, Karen Kim in Chapter Ten provides program descriptions and contact information for readers interested in obtaining more in-depth information about programs for community college leadership development.

You will note that the authors of this volume embody a wealth of practical or scholarly experience or both. This mixture was intentional. We badly need both of these perspectives in the development and execution of top-notch leadership development programming. They lead to a melding of thoughtfulness, creativity, and practicality that will bring the progress we need. We hope you find the articles in this issue stimulating and useful, and if we can be of service, we hope you will contact us directly.

William E. Piland
David B. Wolf
Editors

WILLIAM E. PILAND *is professor of postsecondary education at San Diego State University.*

DAVID B. WOLF *is executive director emeritus, Accrediting Commission for Community and Junior Colleges, Western Association of Schools and Colleges.*

1

All leaders will face difficult circumstances. These will frequently have little or nothing to do with anything the leader created or can influence. Administrators of community colleges, particularly presidents, are commonly neither prepared nor trained to face a tougher, and perhaps meaner, job than in earlier years; those who would lead should understand and be prepared.

Leadership Blues

James G. March, Stephen S. Weiner

A few months before the end of the Second World War, General Tomoyuki Yamashita of the Imperial Japanese Army was sent to the Philippines to take command of the Japanese army there. The military situation was impossible, and within a few months General Yamashita surrendered. One month later, on command of General Douglas MacArthur, he was brought before an American military tribunal (Reel, 1949). The military officers heard testimony that troops under General Yamashita's command had committed atrocities in the Philippines during the final campaign in the islands. The general and his American defense lawyers argued that his army was so disorganized by the attack of allied forces that he did not know of the atrocities and that he could not have done anything about them even if he had known.

Why was General Yamashita brought before the military tribunal? Perhaps it was because he failed to prevent atrocities. Perhaps it was because he had led an attacking force of 30,000 men overland down the Malay Peninsula to capture Singapore and its defending army of 100,000 men early in the war. Perhaps it was because there was anger toward the Japanese in the United States and in the Philippines, and someone had to become a focus for that anger. Perhaps it was because his trial could be a symbol and trophy of General MacArthur's personal power.

It is not easy to make any clear historical assertion about why General Yamashita was brought before the tribunal. But it is not hard to see his experience as a metaphor for the way the joys and angers of others are displaced on leaders. It is a fundamental reality of leadership that it reaps the rewards of public satisfaction and bears the blame for public unhappiness. It matters little whether a leader has done much to create the former or could have

NEW DIRECTIONS FOR COMMUNITY COLLEGES, no. 123, Fall 2003 © Wiley Periodicals, Inc.

done much to prevent the latter. The necessity of social attribution of leader responsibility is an article of faith and an instinct of social behavior. The reputations of all leaders are variations on the reputations of generals.

College and university presidents are not subject to court-martial, nor are they in danger of being executed. But a surprisingly large number feel they have been victims of capricious cruelty at least once in their careers. We have spent a not-inconsiderable portion of our professional lives listening to presidential tales of distress and anxiety, of coping with unexpected turbulence in presidential lives, and of struggling with crises for which presidents were ill prepared and over which they had scant control.

These stories, and the painful experiences that give rise to them, are what we call the "leadership blues." Not all presidents sing the blues, but the odds go up dramatically as the years of presidential tenure increase. One hears these blues not in the confines of a well-upholstered office during business hours but, rather, over a bottle of wine late in the evening or during a long walk on a sandy beach or while on a transcontinental plane flight.

Hearing the blues stirs chords of memory among those who have attempted leadership in similar settings because they capture recurring, important, and often unpleasant features of administrative life in academic organizations. The underlying importance of the blues is what they say about campus culture, civility, and the pleasures and penalties of leadership roles in contemporary colleges. As these matters exert heavy influence over the character of those attracted or repelled by the task of campus leadership, they raise serious questions for American higher education and the society that they serve. We want to understand the blues and, in a later section, to spell out some implications for community college leadership.

The blues arise from experiences that either end a presidency or come close to it:

A president, facing major budgetary problems, proposes to sell some rarely used athletic practice fields to a corporation in search of space to build. The proposal stirs keen opposition, and the resulting firefight features an athletic department, prominent alumni, and several student groups on the attack.

A new president, thinking she has the mandate to organize her office as she sees fit, decides to transfer a presidential assistant, who is Latina, to a job in student services. Shortly after, the disgruntled employee files suit to reverse the transfer, and the campus erupts amidst charges of insensitivity and presidential racism.

At a public college with a collective bargaining agreement with faculty, a president struggles to conclude negotiations over a new contract. The faculty union persists in salary demands that the president believes are far beyond the capacity of the college to pay. The president does not budge, and the faculty vote "no confidence" in the president. The president turns to his board of trustees for support and discovers that the board majority is beholden to the union because of past contributions to their election campaigns.

A president seeking to save money on a building project that is over budget asks his wife, a professional architect, to volunteer her services to trim the project budget. She carries out her task but with little sense of diplomacy. Veteran college officials, believing that the president's action disregards their professional qualifications, deeply resent this intrusion into their domain. The campus is seized by allegations of presidential favoritism and micromanagement, and staff morale sinks.

A president announces the single largest unrestricted gift in the history of her college. As soon as she decides on the allocation of the gift, a broad campus coalition organizes to oppose the president's decision as arbitrary and made without proper consultation on campus. The coalition demands an audience with the board of trustees in public session.

A president suffers under the continuing bitter criticism of a leading member of the board of trustees. The trustee finds no presidential recommendation or decision worthy of support and puts out the word that disaffected members of the college community can bring grievances directly to him. He collects many complaints quickly, in part because of his reputation as the person responsible for the firing of a previous president.

In each of the foregoing cases—and this is but a small sample—the resulting travail lasted for months or years. To be sure, each of these incidents triggered a conflagration because previous events had provided some tinder for the blaze. But for each of the presidents involved, the crisis came as a shock.

Of course, like the story of General Yamashita as told by his lawyer, the blues we have heard come from only the president's point of view. Other people who were involved would tell different stories that speak of different motivations, intentions, and outcomes. Specific events or encounters would read differently if told from another angle of observation. For example, college trustees often play a role in the blues, and when they do, the presidential perspective colors the offending trustees with hues of brashness, personal enmity, ideological passion, simple political ambition, or any subset of these. The trustees would undoubtedly provide a different account that speaks of accountability to the governing board and the difficulties of making entrenched bureaucracies respond.

For anyone who has not endured similar experiences, expressions of pain by leaders might be seen as out of keeping with the old cliché about what happens when the going gets tough or as some kind of sour grapes on the part of those who have been left behind by a competitive world. Such an impression would, however, be misleading. One usually does not hear the blues from the losers in administrative life. It is the survivors who live to sing the blues. In some cases they have survived by dogged persistence, in some cases because their opponents lost interest in the attack, and in other cases by leaving one field of battle for a fresh one on another campus. But they have survived. Their pains are not the excuses of losers but the laments of survivors: laments for a lost dream of an idyllic academic institution, at least as seen by a president.

The blues are full of outrage and hurt. Presidents who sing the blues expected something different. And they expected something better. They anticipated hard work, making tough decisions, and experiencing unpopularity in their professional roles. Leaders of academic institutions have to be ready for such difficulties. They face the challenges posed by the irreverence and indifference of students, the resistance of faculty members who prize their individual and collective autonomy, and the challenges of board members trying to establish their own authority. The college campus has never been an easy place for administrators. But presidents with the blues got far more pain than they bargained for.

Leaders with the blues have encountered worlds that typically contain four features that run through the stories they tell: First, the issues that they confronted were contested with fervor, but they were usually not major issues of educational policy. Rather, the outcomes of campus struggles involve short-term political advantage and some redistribution of power and influence on college campuses—the ebb and flow of careers and fights over keeping and losing jobs.

We learn from the blues that loss of employee morale or trustee confidence is a likely ticket out of town for an administrator, whereas instructional ineffectiveness, stale curricula, or anemic graduation or student transfer rates can often be lost in the noise of campus politics. There are relatively few fights over criteria for faculty hiring or promotion, deep changes in the structure of curricula, or substantial alterations in expectations for student performance. The fundamental educational character of the college is rarely at issue. The most common feature of the conflicts reflected in the blues appears to be jostling for primacy among small groups or individuals or the bumping of one set of career expectations against that of others.

Second, the level of anger and emotion involved in the encounters is out of all proportion to the substantive importance of the issues to which they are explicitly addressed. The criticism voiced by the opposition may be out in the open, or it may be carried in rumors or whispered comments. Presidents are in positions of formal authority (no matter how shaky they may feel), and their enemies, fearful of the power of leaders, are more likely to make hit-and-run guerrilla raids, using gossip and scorn as weapons, than they are to engage in public confrontations. It may be true that the best defense is a good offense, but leaders do not pick the time and circumstances of attacks on them. At the outset of hostilities, these leaders are usually less prepared and less focused than their critics. The blues often carry a sense of ambush—bitterness; personal hatred; tactics of slash and burn; and in the parlance of the current era, "the politics of personal destruction."

A large part of the nastiness that afflicts presidents appears to be the result of symbolic politics, of posturing and attack for the sheer pleasure of being seen on the campus as assertive or as capable of causing grief for persons in positions of leadership. These are not struggles over organizational survival or institutional integrity but local performances arising from anxiety over personal status or the desire to exercise bragging rights. We use these terms not in condemnation of any of the actors in the stories we have heard because, after all, we have heard only one perspective drawn from many-layered dramas. Yet, we can be reasonably sure that when the emotional stakes are high on one side of a controversy, they are likely to be comparably high on all sides.

Third, the levels of trust among participants are low. Paranoia is common and commonly justified. Each president with the blues has a profound sense of being exposed, of the smallest action and least consequential statement being reported and then repeated, often in ways that distort the intended meaning and ignore the context. Loyalty is in doubt. Fears and realizations of betrayal lurk at the edges of the blues. Presidents have a sense that other people stand behind them but, on reflection, they are not sure whether those who stand to their rear are there as friendly forces ready to enter the fray, as potential allies for the enemy, or because there is less heat and controversy toward the rear. Leaders talk about loneliness and a sense of vulnerability: "Where are these attacks coming from, and what is prompting them? Why me?" They recount the need for friendship, for family, and for being connected to a personal life outside of the scene of conflict, incivility, and betrayal. They feel abandoned.

Fourth, the struggles feed on themselves more than they feed on any issues that they involve. There is the sense of being locked in a blood feud, where the original insult, perhaps unintended, is lost from the field of view and all that seems to matter is the next maneuver in a never-ending campaign to gain advantage. The lines of attack and the rhetoric of the opposition can often be traced to old enmities and skirmishes that were assumed to be long forgotten. Thus, memory plays a dual function: On the one hand, it is good for participants in the fight to know "where the bodies are buried" and who played on which team in recent battles. On the other hand, those who carry that knowledge are usually weighted down by lingering resentments and musty grudges that may obscure their view of how the field of contest may have changed in recent years and the fact that old loyalties may no longer be reliable.

A central feature of the leadership blues is a deep mismatch between the conceptions of individual leaders and key features of the organizations they lead. The leaders want to imagine that educational leadership is a noble calling through which people of intelligence and competence come together to guide a united college to shared educational objectives. They want to imagine that issues can be resolved by thoughtful discussion within a community of shared respect. Those imaginations are consistently contradicted by their experience and, if truth be told, often by their own behavior. The organizations they lead are not only fractious, with disagreements over what measures might lead to good educational outcomes, but profoundly torn with respect to their interpretations of educational objectives. They are characterized by low levels of mutual trust. Academic institutions appear to be institutions of human beings with the usual human frailties—pettiness, self-ishness, and sensitivity to imagined insult—frailties that often overcome, or at least obscure, desires to do good.

Over the long run, this mismatch between leader expectations and the reality of educational organizations may well be rectified. Leaders will adjust their conceptions, and education will recruit and retain the leaders it deserves. Along the way, administrators are likely to come to deal more effectively with the worlds in which they find themselves. They will stop having unrealistic expectations about their jobs, their associates, and themselves. Either through training or recruitment, colleges are likely to secure effective educational leaders who can operate under the unpleasant realities of administrative life and even find leaders who enjoy the unpleasantness. Colleges will be led by leaders with few illusions about educational organizations and the people who inhabit them, who accept that there are few shared objectives and little basis for trust, and who thrive in such a world.

The politics of a campus is like the politics of a small town, and presidents need to make deals to accomplish their ends. Even where a college campus is set in a large urban complex, it still usually functions as a small town, living a life largely isolated from the media attention, political power, and civic forces of the city that surrounds it. Thus, we observe the personal, and even petty, politics of a surprisingly small municipality even on a large urban campus. Yet, by and large, college presidents are not trained as politicians, nor do they see themselves as such. Presidents look for allies among faculty, administrators, students or citizens in the surrounding community, and especially among members of their governing boards. But there seems little inclination to try "log-rolling," the trading of support that can serve the highest priority of both presidents and their opponents.

The blues also reveal a persistent dilemma associated with a leader's role in change. As a general rule, one does not enter the "Administrator's Hall of Fame" by presiding over the status quo, no matter how pleasing the current stasis may be for many people associated with the campus, and no matter that any given change may well not be a good idea. The necessity of change is a mantra of leadership, as is the necessity of administrative leadership to effect change. As a result, administrators and other relatively short-term participants in academic life have a persistent bias toward change.

A consistent theme in the blues is the well-intended (but frustrated) initiation of change on the part of those in formal authority. For a new administrator, a driving force is the chance to make a mark on the organization and to build a record of innovative leadership that moves both the campus and the administrator toward their ambitions.

For more experienced members of the college community, the impulse to change on the part of administrators is likely to seem pretentious and self-interested. For them, and especially for the faculty and staff, the advent of a new administrator may simply be another dreary chapter in a long and frustrating story of management gimmicks (for example, management by objectives or continuous quality improvement) and devotion to selfish ambition that, for too long, have provided justification for not listening to those who do vital work every day but who do not reside at the top of the administrative or governance hierarchy. Thus, we can expect on most campuses a severe disagreement about who are true patriots, the genuine adherents of the college's mission. Certainly we can observe on virtually every campus the chasms that separate the faculty from the administration, on the one hand, and the board from the administration, on the other.

These realities of leadership life invite some practical guidelines for college leaders who want to survive in the unpleasant world in which they find themselves. Our recommendation is that anyone who wants to be an administrator should leave his or her innocence behind. The job is not one that produces friends. Because much of the leadership of any institution is bound up in enforcing rules and denying requests, any administrator who wants a friend should buy a dog.

The primary administrative talent is not one of knowing how to make good decisions but of knowing how to manage impressions, making the institutions look good in the eyes of others and creating an illusion of direction and control. Those who sing the blues tell us that it is important to maintain a pretense of confidence and strength, even when feeling uncertain and weak; that it is better to shift attention than to confront criticism; that the best strategy for an ambitious administrator is to depict oneself as the champion of uncontroversial changes to observers on campus (for example, bigger budgets, higher salaries, and nicer buildings) while appearing to eyes outside the campus as having engineered controversial changes in efficiency (reallocating resources, enforcing higher performance standards, cutting budgets to achieve efficiency, and eliminating "deadwood" from staff and faculty).

These guidelines of sophistication and manipulation make a certain amount of sense. By encouraging realistic expectations of leaders, they reduce the gap between expectations and experience. The gap can, however, be reduced in another way—at least in principle. We can change the reality, rather than the leaders' expectations about it.

In the short run, of course, organizational reality adapts relatively slowly, thus inviting changes in the selection and education of leaders. The blues teach us about the powerful feedback mechanism between tactics and mistrust. A tactical reaction to lack of trust may permit survival, but it is a mean survival. It reinforces distrust and traps an organization and its leadership into continual warfare on a terrain of fortresses. In effect, by seeking to train and select leaders who can adapt easily to unattractive worlds they encounter in their roles as leaders, we reduce the likelihood of inducing those worlds to adapt to the kinds of leaders that will ultimately serve us better.

The ability of the community colleges, an extraordinarily important branch of our educational system, to recruit constructive and humane professionals into the various roles of leadership is compromised by the nature of life portrayed here. It is a life from which decent people are likely to be repelled, rejecting the idea of serving as leaders of educational institutions rather than being attracted to the role. We can ask, "How tough, thick-skinned, and even ruthless must community college leaders be to survive in the petty world of campus politics?" If adherence to principles of decency and community is a disadvantage to community college leaders, then will only those without those principles be willing to serve? If so, will this make the community college a less effective instrument of social and individual growth?

The point is not to try to eliminate conflict from colleges, for there are genuine issues on which reasonable people can thoughtfully disagree, but to reduce the destructive personalization and aggravation of conflict and to civilize the culture faced by campus leadership. What can be done?

The issue of civility needs to be placed on the agenda of various groups on campus and statewide associations. What is the reality of the issue? What harm is being done that is of concern to the campus as a whole? What forces are at work? What practical steps can be taken? In this respect, local boards of trustees and the statewide trustee organizations can assume a particular leadership role because they hold ultimate responsibility for the health of the campus, and they should be able to bring a degree of detachment to campus controversies. State-level leaders can also bring attention to the issue as part of the challenge of building trust among state-level constituency groups, and the accrediting commission can insist that civility is a necessary focus for self-study.

Various avenues to build trust and resolve grievances—campus ombudsmen, special campus commissions on human relations, and retreats involving trustees and campus leaders—need to be used more actively. Campuses are well advised to draw on knowledge of conflict resolution techniques within their own faculties and the faculties of nearby institutions.

Campus ceremonies and rituals can be used more widely as occasions for exhibiting mutual recognition and respect. Special days can be designated to recognize the roles of various groups on campus and to celebrate volunteer efforts.

Campus publications can profile individuals and tell their stories of service. Better yet, administrators can write in praise of faculty, and vice versa. Committee assignments and even job sharing can be used as ways to build understanding of the challenges facing leaders on campus.

These are all small steps. They are probably of more use in preventing poisonous conflict than in resolving it. They are undoubtedly romantic in their hopes. In the final analysis, there is no quick fix, and there will be no end to conflict and pettiness. But just as gossip and scorn are effective techniques to demoralize and destroy, mutual respect and recognition are effective techniques to foster unity and the campus coherence necessary to carry on the important work of the community colleges.

Underlying these problems, moreover, are some grander ones. Why is the world of education filled with angry people engaging in gratuitous unpleasantness? Partly, the answer is that modern America has its share of angry people, and education cannot escape being part of that. We live in an incredibly successful and rich society in which many adults react to what seem to be minor insults with vitriol and violence.

But part of the answer lies within the education world and the community college itself. In a series of studies, Roderick M. Kramer (1998) and others have developed a set of ideas about the ways in which suspicions that others are exploiting, harming, or deceiving oneself; doubts about the loyalty and trustworthiness of associates; and fears that information about oneself will be used against oneself lead to a cascade of distrust, sensitivity, and accusation that feed on each other. In Kramer's formulation, paranoid-like reactions are generated not by individual pathologies but by social situations. His studies show how a tendency to attribute events to sinister others acting conspiratorially arises from a feeling that one is under intense evaluative scrutiny that in turn arises from uncertainty about one's social status and a feeling of being different from others involved in the situation. One source of the feeling of being different is an emphasis on separateness rather than unity in a community, hyperconsciousness of the ways in which people in a group differ. One source of uncertainty about one's social status is consciousness of being subordinate in power or authority relations.

In particular, it seems clear that it has become harder for people attached to colleges to see themselves as part of a serious community of similar individuals among whom concerns for the well-being of the institution are important and shared. They are more inclined to define their relations with the college as stemming from relatively narrow definitions of personal or group self-interest and to assume that others are similarly primarily concerned with themselves, thus not to be trusted. Teaching has become less a calling than a job. Administrators have become less reluctant servants of the institution than ambitious careerists. Boards have become less voices of altruistic hopes for learning than the manifestations of particular interests and individual political ambitions.

A vision of a society based on the pursuit of individual and group distinctiveness in pursuit of self-interest is an honorable vision and one that captures an important part of the American spirit, but it has traditionally been combined, particularly in education, with a vision of obligations, community, and mutual civility. There is an obvious tension between the two, and maintaining each as a counterpoint to the other is far from easy. Contemporary American community college life is losing its sense of mission and community, and thereby its civility, to an excess of personal and subgroup differentiation and gratification that generate fears that everyone else is trying to put something over on us.

Most community college presidents were attracted to leadership out of a commitment to the educational and social ideals of the community colleges. Their hard work has brought them knowledge of their institutions as a whole. They have experienced the joy of observing the internal workings of a complex mechanism even if the gears and levers have resisted change and occasionally have injured them seriously. They have made difficult forays into campus politics, have suffered for them, but have survived. They have succeeded in helping individuals in myriad ways. The good news is that idealists persist, and the occasional presidential ogre is detected and fired, either sooner or later.

Leadership blues are a reminder that however much a social system may treasure those who persist in serving the common good in the face of major penalties for doing so, civilization requires civility and will not long survive if its governance attracts only those who are cunning and combative. Leaders will be held accountable for many things over which they have little or no control. That is understood. General Yamashita was executed by the American army on February 23, 1946. But if the daily activities of leadership are corrupted by pettiness and indecency, then only the indecent and petty will find leadership appealing.

References

Kramer, R. M. "Paranoid Cognition in Social Systems: Thinking and Acting in the Shadow of Doubt." *Personality and Social Psychology Review,* 1998, 2, 251–275.
Reel, A. F. *The Case of General Yamashita.* Chicago: University of Chicago Press, 1949.

JAMES G. MARCH is professor emeritus, Stanford University.

STEPHEN S. WEINER is retired executive director, Accrediting Commission for Senior Colleges and Universities, Western Association of Schools and Colleges, and former member of the Board of Governors of California Community Colleges.

2

In this chapter, the author discusses the coming transition in the leadership of America's community colleges, the opportunities and challenges of leadership turnover, the rewards of leadership, and the problems faced by community college leaders. He identifies the skills expected to be necessary for leadership in the twenty-first century and addresses policy implications for leadership preparation.

Leadership Context for the Twenty-First Century

George R. Boggs

The time is growing near for the most significant transition in leadership in the history of America's community colleges. Many of the faculty and administrators who came into the community colleges during the great growth period of the 1960s are approaching retirement. A survey of community college presidents conducted by the American Association of Community Colleges (AACC) in 2001 indicated that 45 percent (*n* = 249) of them planned to retire by 2007 (Shults, 2001). Based on findings from another 2001 survey, Weisman and Vaughan (2002) confirmed that the rate of presidential retirement appears to be on the rise, with 79 percent (*n* = 661) of presidents planning to retire by 2012.

Even more alarming is that the administrators who report to the presidents—and who might be expected to replace them—are also approaching retirement. Whereas the average age of presidents is fifty-six years, that of chief academic officers is fifty-four years, and that of chief student services officers is fifty-two years (Shults, 2001). The community colleges are also losing faculty members. Thirty-five percent (*n* = 249) of the presidents who responded to the 2001 AACC survey projected that 26 percent to 50 percent of their faculty would be retiring between 2001 and 2006. In 1999, 27 percent (*n* = 17,660) of full-time community college faculty members were between the ages of fifty-five and sixty-four years and rapidly approaching retirement (Shults, 2001).

Of course, the coming change is also a window of opportunity to bring greater diversity, new energy, and new ideas to community college faculty and leadership. One of the most encouraging findings of the Weisman and Vaughan survey (2002) was the steady increase in the percentage of female presidents, from 11 percent to 28 percent (*n* = 661) in the past ten years.

NEW DIRECTIONS FOR COMMUNITY COLLEGES, no. 123, Fall 2003 © Wiley Periodicals, Inc.   15

Information collected on new presidents by AACC indicates that this trend toward increased gender diversity in leadership is continuing. Eighty-five (45 percent) of the 189 most recently appointed first-time presidents are women.

However, community colleges have not been as effective as they need to be in diversifying their leadership by ethnicity. The Weisman and Vaughan surveys show only a small increase from 11 percent (n = 837) to 14 percent (n = 680) of presidents who were members of a racial or ethnic minority in the five years between 1991 and 1996. The 2001 survey showed the percentage unchanged at 14 percent (n = 661) (Weisman and Vaughan, 2002).

The question is whether the capacity exists or can be built to prepare new faculty and administrators who are representative of the population, who will understand the unique mission of the community colleges, and who have the skills to lead these institutions into the future. To understand the requirements for community college leadership, it is important first to examine the mission and values of these institutions and the challenges they will face in the future.

Community colleges are a uniquely American invention. Reflecting the democratic ideals of our nation, community colleges have broken with higher education tradition. Their services are shaped by the core values of open access, community responsiveness, resourcefulness, and a clear focus on teaching and learning.

Community colleges have opened access to higher education to people who would not otherwise have that opportunity because of financial or geographical limitations, lack of preparation, or family or job responsibilities. They enroll the most diverse student body in the history of higher education. Their missions are focused on promoting and supporting student learning and do not include requirements for discipline-related research and publication by faculty.

The colleges evolved to be responsive to the educational needs of their communities, offering vocational education programs that are important to communities, contract education for local businesses to prepare and develop their workforces, and community service courses that are important to local community members. Because of financial limitations, college leaders must also be resourceful and readily able to form partnerships with leaders of other educational institutions, business, industry, and government to provide facilities and programs for students. This innovative spirit extends into both the classroom and student service areas, where faculty and staff find creative ways to support students and their learning.

Despite the demonstrated success of community colleges, critics and the uninformed continue to question the community college mission, and community college leaders are continually challenged to defend their core values. Preparing new faculty members and leaders who are committed to the mission and values of community colleges is perhaps the most significant challenge faced by community colleges.

Future Trends for Community Colleges

Effective community college leadership is critical to meeting the societal needs of the twenty-first century. Enrollment in community colleges should continue to increase dramatically in the coming years as children of the "baby boomers" and new immigrants head toward higher education. Moreover, larger percentages of high school graduates are expected to go on to college. In 1979, half of high school graduates attended college. Today, about two-thirds of high school graduates attend college. The U.S. Department of Education (1999) predicts that, by 2009, three-quarters of high school graduates will be going to college. Carnavale and Fry (2000) predict that higher education will have to absorb an additional 2.6 million new students in the twenty years between 1995 and 2015. Much of the increase in enrollment will be from minority and older populations that have been traditionally served by community colleges. The U.S. Department of Education (1999) predicts that an increasing percentage of these new students will be attending community colleges.

The community college role in career preparation should take on even more importance in the years ahead. The Bureau of Labor Statistics has documented a steady increase in skill level required for employment in the United States (Braddock, 1999). This trend is expected to continue. Carnavale and Fry (2000) predict that the percentage of workers with some postsecondary training will increase from 56 percent in 1995 to 76 percent by 2015. Occupations requiring the associate degree are projected to increase faster than occupations requiring any other level of education (Braddock, 1999).

According to the Bureau of Labor Statistics (2000), the median years of job tenure continue to decline. Today's economy requires that skills be updated periodically, sending many people back to school as "lifelong learners." A college degree is no longer seen as a guarantee of job security. In fact, 28 percent of community college noncredit students have a bachelor's degree or higher, and nearly half have some form of postsecondary credential. More than a quarter of the part-time credit students have some form of postsecondary credential.

These societal trends indicate that community colleges will be "where the action is" in higher education in the years ahead. Faculty members and leaders who join community colleges will be able to make significant contributions to educational opportunity and to the economic well-being of individuals and communities.

Rewards of Community College Leadership

Leading these dynamic institutions in a world that has become more complex and demanding presents many challenges. With all of the difficulties of teaching and leadership, it is perhaps best to focus first on why people should want to take on these roles. Writing in the *Chronicle of Higher Education*, Ellen Olmstead (2001) provides an answer:

> People often ask me why I prefer to teach at a community college when I have degrees from the more elite institutions. Why don't I go on and get my Ph.D. and teach at colleges like the ones I attended—where I can enjoy the rewards of more prestige and better pay? In fact, I am honored to have taught my community college students. They make me proud, and they shame me, too, for they have surmounted much greater roadblocks than I ever faced, and their ambitions for themselves make mine for them seem so small. They make it easy to celebrate their successes and hard to forget their struggles. Ours is a labor of love. How can you not embrace that devotion to educational opportunity and, by extension, the environment that solicits and is sustained by it? [p. B-5]

Community college faculty and staff make a difference in the lives of people who may not have other opportunities to pursue a higher education. Tangible evidence of this difference is seen at commencement and program graduation and pinning or capping ceremonies.

Community college faculty and leaders make a real difference for the institutions they serve. College leaders are also often seen as community leaders. Approximately 50 percent (n = 661) of the presidents in the Weisman and Vaughan survey (2002) said they served on boards of corporations or other commercial enterprises. An overwhelming majority (about 93 percent of 661 respondents) said they served on the boards of nonprofit or community-based organizations. Some community college leaders also have an effect on state or national policy through their professional activities. Some have an effect on educational policy and practice through their writing and speaking.

Challenges of Community College Leadership

Although the founding leaders of the community college movement were the pioneers and the builders, today's leaders operate in a more complex world. Resources are constrained, accountability requirements are increasing, labor relations are becoming more contentious, and society is more litigious than ever before. Learning opportunities and services are now expected to be offered twenty-four hours a day, seven days a week. Distance-learning technologies are erasing geographical boundaries, and competition for students is increasing.

College leaders are expected to respond ever more quickly to meet emerging community and national needs. Community colleges are being asked to respond to the shortage of health care workers and teachers, to help bridge the "digital divide," and to prepare students to live in an increasingly global society and economy.

The respondents to the 2001 AACC presidential survey revealed that they were not prepared for several aspects of community college leadership (Shults, 2001). They were not prepared for the overwhelming demands of the job. Community college leadership can be all-consuming, and the more responsibility one has, the more time it takes to do a good job. Weisman and Vaughan (2002) found that presidents perform official duties in the evenings, on weekends, and while on vacation. Because of the time commitment, presidents revealed difficulty in balancing their professional, private, and spiritual lives. Ten percent (n = 661) of the presidents in the Weisman and Vaughan survey (2002) have commuter marriages, further complicating their personal lives.

Presidents reported being "lonely at the top." Because faculty members and midlevel administrators always have peers at the institution who are doing almost the same job, there are others from whom to seek advice and with whom to commiserate. But there is only one president. At the same time that presidents report being alone, they are also very visible, recognized and set apart by the uniqueness of their position.

Relationship building is an important part of a leader's responsibilities. To advance the mission of the college, it is essential to have the active support of all college constituencies. External relationships can give the college support in the form of resources, facilities, and good will. However, many presidents reported being unprepared to deal with both internal and external relationships.

Fundraising and financial management were two skills for which presidents reported a lack of preparation. Because community colleges are the most insufficiently financed institutions of American higher education, it is important for the presidents to understand increasingly complex fiscal principles. College leaders do not have the luxury of making financial mistakes. Community college leaders are not as experienced as their colleagues in other sectors of higher education in raising private funds. With projections of declining public revenues for colleges, these skills will be more important.

Presidents reported being unprepared for their work with governing boards. In fact, stories of problems between presidents and boards abound. Sometimes presidents look for ways to survive their boards rather than seeing themselves and their boards as teams that provide direction to a complex enterprise.

All too often, community college faculty and leaders are subjected to incivility within their campus communities. Leaders, in particular, are sometimes subjected to excessive criticism and, occasionally, harassment. It has somehow become acceptable to attack campus leaders, whether they are faculty members or administrators. Perhaps this has been caused by governance struggles, difficult labor negotiations, or autocratic behavior. Whatever the cause, faculty and leaders must learn how to improve the climate on community college campuses.

Leadership and faculty development programs and institutes must do a better job of preparing people to meet the challenges of leadership. What we know about the problems that current leaders are facing should be a guide for developing the curriculum needed for institutes, mentorships, and doctoral programs.

Essential Leadership Skills for the Twenty-First Century

In its 2001 survey, AACC asked presidents to identify the most important skills for future leaders. Responses included financial planning "know-how," the ability to forge partnerships, the ability to improve and maintain relationships within and outside the college, the ability to develop a "clear vision," excellent communication skills, political savvy, and adaptability (Shults, 2001). Weisman and Vaughan (1997) identified a complementary list of important leadership skills in their 1996 survey, including the ability to bring the college together in governance, the ability to mediate, a good command of technology, a high tolerance for ambiguity, understanding and appreciating multiculturalism, and an ability to build coalitions. The AACC Board Task Force on Leadership Development (AACC, 2002) identified the following essential leadership skills: understanding and implementing the community college mission; effective advocacy skills; administrative skills; community and economic development skills; and personal, interpersonal, and transformational skills.

Future community college leaders must be models of integrity, honesty, and high ethical standards. They must be open to new ideas, and their judgments must be fair, dispassionate, and equitable. They must confront issues and people without prejudice. In particular, they must ensure that students are respected as individual learners and protected from disparagement, embarrassment, or capricious behavior. They must realize that retaining their popularity is not as important as doing what is right.

To be successful in today's environment and that of the future, leaders must find ways to involve people in their decisions. They must be catalysts for finding ways to make things happen for the college and its people. They should encourage and support innovation and discovery (Boggs, 1995).

Future leaders will be selected because of their demonstrated knowledge and skills. They will need opportunities to learn, to develop, and to practice these skills through simulations, internships, and mentorships. Leadership programs should be structured to provide these opportunities for skill development.

Status of Leadership Preparation and Training Programs

Shults (2001) reported a 78 percent decline in the number of advanced degrees in community college administration from 1982–83 to 1996–97. In fact, few of the Kellogg-funded Community College Leadership Programs started in the 1960s have been sustained. However, AACC has documented that there are 140 university-based degree programs that have at least some coursework in the community college (http://www.aacc.nche.edu). Moreover, within the past few years, several community college programs have been established or reestablished.

AACC has also catalogued thirty short-term, nondegreed leadership development programs (http://www.aacc.nche.edu). Many of these are offered by the councils affiliated with AACC, but others are offered by universities, states, and organizations such as the League for Innovation in the Community College (Executive Leadership Institute) and the National Institute for Leadership Development. AACC itself is offering a Future Leader Institute that began in 2003.

Leadership Recruitment

The AACC board of directors has asked its association to assist the nation's community colleges in the recruitment of new faculty and leaders. In response, AACC staff members have initiated or are in the process of initiating recruitment-related services. For some time, AACC has provided the opportunity for colleges to advertise their position openings in the *Community College Times,* a bimonthly newspaper that reaches all member colleges, individual subscribers, and many other educational institutions. AACC has extended this service to its new Web Career Center, allowing colleges to recruit on the Web.

Association staff members are planning to initiate a preconvention career exposition that would be held in conjunction with the annual AACC convention. This job fair will give colleges the opportunity to disseminate information about openings and to interact with or interview potential applicants. Sessions are planned to help develop strategies for selecting the applicants that best meet the colleges' needs. Sessions for applicants will help develop application and interviewing skills.

Association staff members are also examining the potential for opening an AACC service to help colleges recruit faculty, staff, and administrators. At this early stage, the association hopes to offer a menu of recruitment services that will fit the particular needs of member colleges. The menu could include training for search committees, candidate reference checking, or full search services from beginning to employment.

Leadership Development and Preparation

The AACC Board Leadership Development Task Force was interested in expanding opportunities for preparing new leaders. For several years, AACC has offered preconvention workshops for aspiring presidents to help them prepare for the presidency and to help them with interviewing and application skills. In 2002, AACC staff members catalogued the university-based degree programs and short-term leadership development institutes and have listed these programs on the AACC Web site.

Short-term leadership development institutes and other AACC initiatives can help meet the need to prepare new leaders. However, the best way to affect leadership development may be to encourage individual community colleges to offer leadership development programs for their own faculty and staff. Some excellent examples of college-based leadership development programs sponsored by college presidents include programs at Parkland College in Champaign, Illinois, Guilford Technical College in Greensboro, North Carolina, and Daytona Beach Community College in Florida. Similarly, some states, including Louisiana, Missouri, and Kentucky, have now established state-level community college leadership development programs, usually under the sponsorship of the state director or chancellor of the community college system. These programs often include sessions on state system or college history and values and information on state and national education policy questions. Every president and chancellor should come to understand that part of the job is to develop the next generation of community college leaders. To encourage this practice, AACC offers sessions at its Presidents Academy Summer Institute on developing locally based leadership development programs.

Mentoring programs are an effective way to inspire and prepare future leaders. Fifty-seven percent (n = 249) of the presidents responding to the 2001 AACC survey reported that mentors had been either valuable or very valuable in helping them obtain their current presidency. Sixty-two percent reported that mentors had been either valuable or very valuable in preparing them for the daily challenges and tasks of the presidency (Shults, 2001). One long-established mentoring program for community college leaders is supported by the Association of California Community College Administrators.

Fortunately, presidents are reaching out to help others. Seventy-six percent of the CEOs who had been in their positions for more than three years had served as a formal mentor (Shults, 2001). Amey and VanDerLinden (2002) found in their study of the career paths of senior community college administrators (n = 910) that 56 percent had mentors. However, only about 43 percent had participated in a career review to plan ways to acquire additional skills, education, or training.

AACC Leadership Support

AACC has a long history of providing support for incumbent community college presidents and chancellors through its Presidents Academy Summer Institute (PASI). PASI gives community college leaders an opportunity to learn and to develop a network of support in a relaxed environment. The D.C. Institute provides an opportunity for a small group of presidents to come to the nation's Capitol to hear from policymakers and representatives of the media. The Technology Institute encourages presidents to bring teams from their institutions to learn about the latest uses of technology in supporting teaching and learning and institutional processes. PASI also sponsors programs at the AACC and Association of Community College Trustees conventions.

Although PASI and convention presentations are designed to provide current information for presidents and to help in their leadership development, perhaps the most valuable aspect is to help leaders develop a supportive network. It is a great value to understand that other people are struggling with the same issues and to know that there is someone to call for advice.

AACC also supports leaders with its convention and conference programming, teleconferences on emerging issues, and practical publications such as *Balancing the Presidential Seesaw* (Vaughan, 2000), *Before Crisis Hits: Building a Strategic Crisis Plan* (Smith and Miller, 2002), and *Public Relations and the Presidency* (Ross and Halstead, 2001). The bimonthly *Community College Journal*, the biweekly *Community College Times*, and a biweekly electronic AACC letter to member presidents provide both news and supportive information. An expanded preconvention workshop for new presidents was initiated in 2003. Past preconvention workshops have focused on such issues as crisis planning and dealing with the media.

AACC recently concluded a research project on CEO employment contracts with the publication of *The CEO Employment Contract: A Guide for Presidents and Boards* (Wallin, 2003), which outlines provisions that should be included in an employment contract. The AACC also conducted a survey of CEO salaries and benefits in 2002 to help presidents and boards when negotiating employment conditions. The publication of the research brief on CEO compensation is in progress.

AACC has been working with the Association of Community College Trustees to develop an expanded service to provide workshops and advice to college trustees and CEOs. The intent is to give colleges a menu of services, including confidential assessments, recommendations, and retreats, that help to keep operations running smoothly and that improve the level of trust between boards and CEOs.

Policy Implications

For institutions that are dedicated to the learning and development of people, community colleges often do not give enough attention to developing their own faculty, staff, and leaders. If community colleges are to develop the skills needed for effective teaching, student services, and leadership, professional development programs must be expanded and improved. Trustees and college leaders should see to it that every college has a sufficient budget for staff and professional development. Travel to conferences, workshops, and institutes should be supported. Sabbatical leave policies should be developed to allow for graduate study in leadership development. Sadly, support for these activities is all too often unavailable.

Because college employees are usually focused on meeting current needs for students and the institution, it often falls to the trustees to insist on policies that prepare for the future. Boards and CEOs should do a policy audit to identify the ways that the college supports the development of its faculty, staff, and leaders. Policy shortcomings that are identified should be addressed.

Sometimes trustees and CEOs question the use of limited resources to provide development opportunities to individuals who will probably leave the institution for another leadership opportunity. However, even if an employee does eventually leave the college for another position, that person is more likely to be productive and dedicated in an environment that supports growth. In the long run, the college will be the beneficiary of support provided by another college when it hires someone from outside the institution. Wise college policymakers will embrace a larger view of employee development.

State policymakers also have a role in meeting the need for new leaders and faculty. State legislators and governors should ensure that there is sufficient financial support from the state for professional development programs. All too often, state policymakers fail to recognize the importance of professional development, and these programs may lose support during periods of fiscal exigency. However, a growing number of directors and chancellors of state community college systems are offering leadership development programs for promising faculty members and administrators in their colleges, most recently in Kentucky and Louisiana.

Conclusion

The turnover in faculty and leadership of the nation's community colleges should be seen as both an opportunity and a challenge. It is an opportunity for new people to bring new energy, new direction, and new ideas into the community colleges. The challenge is to preserve the mission and values of the community colleges and to prepare faculty and leaders to be successful in a more complex environment. Recent research studies have documented the need to prepare future leaders and have identified skills that future leaders will need to be successful. The leaders of state systems, university professors in community college programs, and community college associations, councils, and organizations all have roles to play in the development of future faculty and leaders. One of the most important roles can be played by college presidents and chancellors who should understand that faculty and leadership development is one of their most critical responsibilities.

References

American Association of Community Colleges. "Effective Community College Presidents." [http://www.aacc.nche.edu/Content/NavigationMenu/ResourceCenter/Leadership_Programs/Professional_Development.htm]. Nov. 8, 2002.

Amey, M. J., and VanDerLinden, K. E. *Career Paths for Community College Leaders.* Washington, D.C.: Community College Press, 2002.

Boggs, G. R. "The President and the Executive Leadership Team: Solving Strategic Problems." In G. A. Baker III and Assoc. (eds.), *Team Building for Quality*. Washington, D.C.: Community College Press, 1995.

Braddock, D. "Occupational Employment Projections to 2008." *Monthly Labor Review*, 1999, *122*(11), 51–77.

Bureau of Labor Statistics. *Employee Tenure in 2000*. USDL 00–245. Washington, D.C.: U.S. Department of Labor, Aug. 29, 2000.

Carnavale, A. P., and Fry, R. A. *Crossing the Great Divide*. Princeton, N.J.: Education Testing Service, 2000.

Olmstead, E. "It's the Community-College Life for Me." *Chronicle of Higher Education*, May 25, 2001, p. B-5.

Ross, J. E., and Halstead, C. P. *Public Relations and the Presidency*. Washington, D.C.: Community College Press, 2001.

Shults, C. *The Critical Impact of Impending Retirements on Community College Leadership*. Washington, D.C.: Community College Press, 2001.

Smith, L., and Miller, D. *Before Crisis Hits: Building a Strategic Crisis Plan*. Washington, D.C.: Community College Press, 2002.

U.S. Department of Education. *Digest of Educational Statistics, 1998*. (NCES) Washington, D.C.: U.S. Department of Education, 1999.

Vaughan, G. B. *Balancing the Presidential Seesaw*. Washington, D.C.: Community College Press, 2000.

Wallin, D. *The CEO Contract: A Guide for Presidents and Boards*. Washington, D.C.: Community College Press, 2003.

Weisman, I. M., and Vaughan, G. B. *The Community College Presidency at the Millennium*. Washington, D.C.: Community College Press, 1997.

Weisman, I. M., and Vaughan, G. B. *The Community College Presidency 2001*. Washington, D.C.: Community College Press, 2002.

GEORGE R. BOGGS *is the president and chief executive officer of the American Association of Community Colleges.*

3

The authors consider the current need for faculty leadership, the motivation to lead, and the challenges and problems faculty encounter in their leadership roles and provide a sampling of leadership development initiatives across the nation.

Developing Community College Faculty as Leaders

Joanne E. Cooper, Louise Pagotto

That there is a crisis in community college leadership is not news. The alarm was sounded in the western region in 1998, when a group of community college leaders met to voice their concerns (Community College Leadership Development Initiatives at Claremont Graduate University, 2000; Hernandez, 2001). More recently, Shults (2001) has painted a somber picture of the national leadership scene. At a time when the responsibilities of community college leaders require a skill set and knowledge base more complex than ever before, when the average age of senior administrators is rising, and when almost half of current presidents expect to retire in the next five years, the number of graduate degrees awarded in community college administration has plummeted. Furthermore, in a study of community college leadership preparation, Brown, Martinez, and Daniel (2002) surveyed three hundred community colleges leaders about their perceptions of the adequacy of their doctoral programs in higher education leadership. Responses from 128 instructional leaders indicate a disconnect between the skills and knowledge emphasized in graduate programs and the skills and knowledge today's leaders felt were most necessary for effective leadership. Given the current demographic trends and the focus of established doctoral leadership programs, graduate programs alone may not fill the need for leaders in community colleges. Vaughan (2001) suggests three avenues for preparing future community college leaders: that funding be increased through the American Association of Community Colleges (AACC) to support the development of potential leaders; that relevant graduate programs be designed through collaborative efforts involving college

NEW DIRECTIONS FOR COMMUNITY COLLEGES, no. 123, Fall 2003 © Wiley Periodicals, Inc.

presidents, AACC, foundations, and graduate professors; and that current presidents give serious consideration to the pool of potential leaders on their campuses. It is to this third option that we now turn.

Whether they enter leadership opportunities with or without previous experience in leadership training and development programs, new community college leaders are often drawn from faculty ranks. They may have well-developed teaching skills but not necessarily the requisite leadership skills. Often faculty do not make conscious choices to step into leadership, but instead find themselves drawn in because of their expertise or their influence on others. In many ways, these individuals may be most in need of leadership development programs, as they suddenly find themselves floundering in new roles for which they are unprepared. In this chapter, we address the reasons why community college faculty step into these roles, the challenges and problems they encounter in these roles, their leadership training and development needs, and existing policies and training programs specific to community college leadership.

Sources of Leadership

Past conceptions of leadership as residing in particular individuals or roles have slowed the emergence of leaders because faculty often see themselves as lacking innate abilities or not inhabiting formal administrative roles. More recent conceptions of leadership reflect the understanding that it is not an individual trait but is manifest throughout an educational community. Thus, leadership can be understood as separate from any particular role or person and providing opportunities for all organizational members. This conception supports the notion that leadership is the engagement of all in the construction of meanings that lead toward a common organizational purpose (Lambert and others, 2002).

Leadership can then be defined much more broadly as the capacity to influence others. According to Gardner (1995), leaders are "individuals who significantly influence the thoughts, behaviors and/or feelings of others" (p. 6). This broad definition includes faculty in all positions throughout the organization, in the classroom, directing committee work, serving as department chairs, and the like.

Community college faculty may influence others through work on various committees such as a faculty hiring committee or through formal leadership roles such as academic senate chair. Faculty may be asked to lead searches for both faculty and administrative positions; to serve on or chair curriculum committees, budget committees, or promotion and tenure committees; and to hold union leadership roles and various other temporary or permanent positions while maintaining full-time faculty status. Faculty may also be called on to step into managerial roles such as dean, director, or division head. These positions are often interim or acting initially, but with time and experience, faculty may move into permanent administrative positions or perhaps move in and out of administrative and faculty roles throughout their careers. Movement in and out of leadership roles is fluid and exists on a continuum of influence, rather than in fixed and rigid positions. Jean Lipman-Blumen (1996) asserts that current conditions in the world call for "more leaders at every organizational and community level," with a resulting increased "need for so-called ordinary people to learn the dynamics of leadership" (p. 116).

Given these various forces, faculty often feel the pull of leadership from the moment they enter community colleges, a pull that usually increases as they become more senior in their departments and divisions. They often move from roles on committees and senates into positions such as department or division chairs, deans, or provosts as their careers progress. However, given the graying of the senior faculty, who are preparing to retire in record numbers in the next five years (Shults, 2001), the mantle of leadership will increasingly fall on junior faculty, underscoring an even greater need for appropriate leadership development among this sector of the campus community. Unfortunately, for many community college faculty members, leadership is not perceived as a particularly attractive position.

Motivation to Lead

The negative perceptions of the consequences of leadership and the challenges faced by those individuals who take on leadership mitigate against ever filling the imminent leadership void. Whatever would possess a faculty member to go over to the "dark side" under these conditions? "Sheer masochistic insanity" was the answer given by one faculty participant at the recent Community College Leadership Development Initiatives (CCLDI) Leadership Academy. The academy is described in detail in Chapter Eight.

Faculty members attending the leadership academy responded to a survey asking what motivated them to step into leadership positions. For some faculty members, the leadership opportunity came to them by default as a result of a leadership void at their institution or, in the words of one participant, being "the only one who couldn't say 'no.'" For others, the opportunity to learn more about their institution was a welcomed challenge. They saw the movement in terms of their own career goals, as a prelude to a greater decision-making role and a desire to move up to more influential leadership positions. Still others took on the challenges as a result of their commitment to their institution. They were inspired by a desire to contribute to or serve their institution, to "bring change and innovation," or to make a difference.

Across the Pacific in Hawaii, sixteen faculty members participated in a leadership training workshop at Kapi'olani Community College in Honolulu in the summer of 2002. They represented the institution's leaders, both direct (department chairs and unit heads) and indirect (union leaders and program coordinators). These participants were also asked why they had chosen to take on leadership roles. Not surprisingly, their answers were similar to those provided by faculty attendees at the CCLDI Leadership Academy. They wanted to give back to the institution, and they saw leadership opportunities as a "natural progression" in their careers. Nevertheless, some Kapiʻolani responses differed from those of the CCLDI participants. Two of the Kapiʻolani faculty noted that they actually enjoyed leadership and the control it afforded them. Others wanted to "take a break" from their current duties and to reinvent themselves. The new positions brought others opportunities to use the knowledge they had gained in their previous roles, to learn something new, and to see their institution from a larger perspective.

However, almost half of the faculty in both the CCLDI and Kapiʻolani groups were in leadership positions because they had been invited to take on these roles by their peers or, most often, administrators. The prevalence of personal invitation as the pathway to leadership confirms and highlights the vital role of today's leaders in identifying and developing their successors.

Leadership Challenges

In a survey given to community college faculty, senior administrators, classified staff, and trustees at the CCLDI Leadership Academy, constituents reported a variety of problems or challenges encountered by faculty. Faculty report struggles to balance their teaching and nonteaching responsibilities; problems motivating others to volunteer their time; and challenges in understanding issues of organizational structure, power, and budgets. They often have a need to see the organization from a larger perspective as they move from their classrooms into more formal bureaucratic structures. As one faculty member reported, "There is a need to understand" who has the power to make decisions "and give permission for change."

Challenges come at the personal as well as the organizational level. One faculty member reported feeling "stark, abject terror" when stepping into a leadership role. Faculty simply may not have the training or the expertise needed when they assume initial leadership roles.

Administrators, trustees, and staff see an even larger array of problems and challenges faculty encounter as they step into leadership roles. These observers of faculty underscore the need for faculty to see the big picture or the changing nature of the larger organization. Faculty are challenged to build and maintain credibility with their colleagues and to work against perceptions in others that they have "sold out." The concerns about credibility and selling out are echoed in Shugart's (1999) assertion that trust is the bedrock of effective leadership. He underscores the need for leaders who are open and nondefensive with well-developed habits of listening and serving. This concern can also be seen in Vaughan's (2000) case studies of community college presidents. He asserts that a sure way for a president to lose his or her balance is to lie to or mislead the faculty. Given this reality in the case studies of presidents, it is not surprising that faculty stepping into leadership roles suddenly face questions about their credibility.

Faculty will find both benefits and challenges from their work as leaders. New leadership roles can add to faculty vitality (Blond and Schmitz, 1988) but in the long run may also lead to burnout (Wubbels, 2002). Although stress and emotional dysfunction are possible outcomes of leadership work (Schell, 1999), the benefits of faculty taking on leadership roles are many, both for individuals in need of renewal and for institutions that need reenergized faculty in order to meet institutional goals and create organizational change. Lipman-Blumen (1996) asserts that leaders help their constituents engage in life-expanding experiences by articulating and legitimizing grand purposes. Stepping into leadership roles can itself be a life-expanding experience for faculty, thus renewing their vitality, creating new challenges, and fostering their growth and development. The positive outcomes of leadership can best be achieved by properly preparing faculty for these new roles.

Leadership Development Initiatives

Effective leadership in this century will be focused on building and sustaining collaborative relationships between increasingly diverse stakeholders and balancing the tensions between the interdependence that is necessary for meaningful collaboration and the politics of difference that is the context for these relationships (Lipman-Blumen, 1996). In community colleges, these connections must be forged between constituencies that have become increasingly adversarial in an environment where the institutional mission may have become less focused and where financial resources are shrinking. This is not the ideal situation for building connections. It is, therefore, not surprising that faculty and administrators at the CCLDI Leadership Academy identified conflict management as an important component of leadership development training. In fact, conflict management was the item most often mentioned as a leadership need. This perception is mirrored in the national study by Brown, Martinez, and Daniel (2002) in which respondents also gave priority to "conflict resolution, mediation, and negotiation skills" in their ranking of forty-eight needed skills for community college leaders.

For most other leadership training needs, the faculty and administrators at the CCLDI Leadership Academy had different perceptions. Faculty respondents focused on specific leadership needs: institutional terminology, Roberts' Rules of Order, and an understanding of the budget process. Administrators, on the other hand, identified the connective aspects of leadership: group facilitation, team building, working with multiple constituencies, and viewing situations through multiple lenses "because a bigger picture will emerge which will foster creativity."

These CCLDI participants agreed that an important part of leadership development is to foster faculty's awareness of the possible effects of their new roles on their collegial relationships and their relationships with other campus stakeholders. In the words of one administrator, leadership development should include "training in understanding political economies and their effect on institutional choices" and "learning to work in teams—seeing the world from an institutional versus discipline perspective." In making decisions as campus leaders, faculty need to weigh "multiple variables among multiple departments." In implementing decisions, faculty need training in "building and supporting high-performing teams." To be effective, leaders must nurture the talents of their colleagues and members of other constituent groups. Faculty leaders must learn to "clarify and ennoble the role of all constituent groups at the table" to promote active, authentic participation and decrease the defensiveness that often occurs when difficult decisions must be made. Leadership development programs should also address the affective needs of faculty by integrating activities and training that bolster faculty's self-confidence and self-esteem, that nurture innovation and risk taking, and that assist faculty in developing strategies to "sustain [themselves] through difficult times."

Opportunities for Faculty Leadership Development

Opportunities for leadership development are varied and extensive. Fostering leadership potential and entrée into the broader institutional culture through mentoring relationships with current leaders was noted by both faculty and administrators at the CCLDI Leadership Academy as an important component of leadership development. Formal and informal mentoring programs are in place in many community colleges. The outcomes most often noted in discussions of mentoring programs are renewal of senior faculty and acculturation and retention of junior faculty. However, as Luna and Cullen (1995) point out, what is missing is an analysis of effective strategies and an assessment of the outcomes of mentoring programs for all stakeholders: the mentors, the new faculty, and the institution.

Formal degree programs in higher education leadership also offer faculty the option of acquiring requisite leadership skills. Some programs focus specifically on community college leadership. For example, the University of Texas at Austin offers the Community College Leadership Program, which is said to be "the nation's oldest graduate program with a primary focus on the preparation of key community college leaders." The nation's most recent addition to formal programs in leadership is likely to be the efforts by the CCLDI to promote faculty development, described elsewhere in this volume. In addition to the oldest and the newest programs, a number of other degree programs in community college leadership are available. The database at AACC's Web site includes a state-by-state listing of such graduate programs (see also Chapter Ten for an annotated list of programs).

Brown, Martinez, and Daniel (2002) assert that leadership development at the institutional level is an especially effective mechanism for addressing the particular needs of any community college because "[o]n-site leadership training can take into consideration the characteristics and traits of the leader, characteristics of the led, context or situation, structure, goals, location, training and ability of subordinates, motivation, organizational culture, size of organization, communication patterns, economics, politics, and other external influences" (p. 63). Moreover, localized programs are more likely to develop the faculty leaders who are best suited for the institutional context in which they will serve. Two such on-site leadership development efforts are presented below.

Two Leadership Training Models

The following question remains: how do we best design and deliver leadership development programs so that faculty can both lead and maintain collegial relationships? Two programs recently developed in Hawaii may provide interesting models.

One effort, which was part of the western region-wide effort of CCLDI, provided intensive leadership development to a single campus: Honolulu Community College. Nineteen faculty and administrators, all identified as having leadership abilities and potential, attended a four-day institute in July 2001. Leadership topics covered during the institute included communication skills, systems thinking, empowering and limiting beliefs, power, building teams, and leading change. As a follow-up, each participant created an action plan with a set of concrete actions identified to reach a clearly defined goal. Each participant was assigned an executive coach to meet with during the following six months to help with the fulfillment of the action plan. To provide lasting changes, the participants were also assigned to a team that would form a support network back on their campus. These teams met regularly throughout the following academic year to support each other's efforts to create change on the campus. Both the coaches and the meetings with their team members that followed the institute were cited in an evaluation conducted the next spring as important parts of the experience. Faculty described the efforts to bring key members of the organization together both for the institute and the meetings during the year as allowing for the development of a core group of "can-do" people who have continued to make change in the college. Seventy-eight percent of the participants reported that they felt an improved capacity for leadership given this experience. They reported being aware of their own strengths and weaknesses; they had a better idea of what motivated others on campus and a better understanding of the need to be more vocal and to take risks.

An observer-evaluator enlisted from Claremont Graduate University in Claremont, California, also provided valuable feedback on the institute.

Initial feedback indicated that faculty valued the opportunity to reflect with their colleagues on the meaning of their work. They came away with a stronger commitment "to actively participate in the process of change" on their campus, a deeper sense of purpose, and a greater appreciation of the dedication of their colleagues. Future leadership development opportunities are planned for other campuses in the system.

A second effort is a systemic, statewide coordination of leadership development on seven community college campuses in Hawaii. The Wo Learning Champions initiative was instituted in December 2000 through the University of Hawaii Community Colleges with support from an endowment funded by the James and Juanita Wo Foundation and the Robert and Betty Wo Foundation. The foundations have pledged $1 million over five years. The chancellor for the University of Hawaii Community Colleges and selected administrators designed the basic structure of the group and the overall responsibilities of the campus representatives. Each of the seven community colleges and the Employment Training Center selects one individual in the institution who has demonstrated a commitment to putting learning first and shown leadership in sharing these innovations with others. These eight individuals, the Wo Learning Champions, are given a modest stipend to be used for their own professional and leadership development and meet monthly to coordinate activities that move the state's community colleges and Employment Training Center in the same direction: promoting effective learning and developing effective leaders. Each of the activities conducted by the Wo Learning Champions is evaluated by participants, and overall assessment has been included as part of the program design.

The first eight Wo Learning Champions (2001–02) were responsible for developing a range of potential program activities. They also conducted a two-day seminar for eighteen mostly junior faculty members from all eight institutions. The spring 2002 seminar focused on sharing effective strategies for promoting learning, identifying leadership opportunities on each campus, and committing to an action plan for the following year. After their eighteen months of service as Wo Learning Champions, the first generation of representatives has returned to their campuses to continue their efforts and to nurture the efforts of their colleagues. The second generation of Wo Learning Champions (2002–03) has since been selected and continues to promote leadership and professional development as part of their eighteen-month assignment. This time, the focus is on virtual communities of practice. Through the development of online resources and a systemwide online mentoring program, the second generation has broadened the effects of professional development across all campuses and made it possible for faculty to develop their leadership potential through electronic channels. These champions have also planned the first Wo Learning Champions Distinguished Lecturer presentation for fall 2003.

The alienation that faculty sometimes feel when they take on leadership roles is minimized by the Wo Learning Champions' absolute focus on the needs of their colleagues. The first activity conducted by the Wo Learning Champions in spring 2001 was an assessment of the professional development needs on each of their campuses. This compilation of needs became the basis for the activities that have been planned thus far. The Wo Learning Champions function on their campuses as advocates for leadership and professional development. For instance, in spring 2003, the Wo Learning Champion from Leeward Community College in Pearl City, Hawaii, coordinated a half-day series of workshops, the Innovations Institute, where colleagues shared effective teaching strategies. They have the opportunity to effect change across all the institutions in the state while developing their own leadership potential. A strength of this approach to leadership development is that the program is designed by faculty for faculty.

Policy Implications

Taking into account the retirement statistics of today's leaders and the crucial role of leadership development for the faculty who will be asked to step into the many vacancies in leadership positions, it may be time for community colleges to examine the need for institutional policies related to leadership training. Should training programs for new faculty leaders be mandatory? The benefits of such a policy are obvious: leaders who would be better prepared to lead, empowered with effective strategies for the demands of connective leadership, and strengthened by enhanced skills. The financial and human resources necessary to provide mandatory leadership development programs are clearly prohibitive for individual institutions to undertake. However, regional or other consortia may be the most feasible vehicles for delivering these training opportunities. Technology allows any number of institutions to share Web-based training materials and to create virtual learning communities, avenues that could enhance leadership development opportunities in community colleges that otherwise do not have the resources to provide such training.

Community colleges need to reexamine other leadership-related policies as well. Faculty often cycle in and out of leadership positions. In some cases, their service in administrative capacities negatively affects their time in rank necessary to apply for promotion. Thus, faculty who have served as administrators and have returned to faculty ranks may find themselves unable to use their successes as leaders in subsequent applications for promotion as faculty members. In other cases, faculty who show exceptional promise are invited to serve in leadership roles early in their careers before they are granted tenure. These promising leaders need to be protected from the possible repercussions of unpopular decisions they may have made while serving as leaders.

Conclusion

As the crisis in leadership for the community colleges of our nation deepens, the need for a willing core of new leaders who are prepared for the challenges they will face becomes even greater. Faculty must begin to understand that leadership is manifest throughout our educational communities and does not reside exclusively in particular individuals or roles. From this vantage point, faculty form the base on which community college education takes place and are potential participants in leadership roles. Colleges must provide motivation and support for faculty to develop leadership potential. Although faculty who answer this call to leadership face problems and challenges, they will also find support in the current programs developing leadership capacity across the nation. Ultimately, faculty have been and will be the most significant source of leadership talent for community colleges. Leadership development programs and local policy should be focused on this constituency.

References

Blond, C., and Schmitz, C. "Faculty Vitality on Review: Retrospect and Prospect." *Journal of Higher Education,* 1988, *59*(2), 190–224.

Brown, L., Martinez, M., and Daniel, D. "Community College Leadership Preparation: Needs, Perceptions, and Recommendations." *Community College Review,* 2002, *30*(1), 45–66.

Community College Leadership Development Initiatives at Claremont Graduate University. *Meeting New Leadership Challenges in the Community Colleges.* Claremont, Calif.: Community College Leadership Development Initiatives at Claremont Graduate University, 2000.

Gardner, H., with Laskin, E. *Leading Minds: An Anatomy of Leadership.* New York: Basic Books, 1995.

Hernandez, J. "Dancing on a Moving Rug." In *Profiles for Progress: Preparing Community College Leaders for a New Era.* Report no. 2. Claremont, Calif.: Community College Leadership Development Initiatives at Claremont Graduate University, 2001.

Lambert, L., and others. *The Constructivist Leader.* (2nd ed.) New York: Teachers College Press, 2002.

Lipman-Blumen, J. *Connective Leadership: Managing in a Changing World.* Oxford, U.K.: Oxford University Press, 1996.

Luna, G., and Cullen, D. L. *Empowering the Faculty: Mentoring Redirected and Renewed.* ASHE-ERIC Higher Education Report no. 3. Washington, D.C.: Graduate School of Education and Human Development, George Washington University, 1995.

Schell, B. H. *Management in the Mirror: Stress or Emotional Dysfunction in Lives at the Top.* Westport, Conn.: Quorum, 1999.

Shugart, S. C. "A Brief Philosophy of Community College Leadership." Orlando, Fla.: Valencia Community College, 1999. (ED 445 729)

Shults, C. *The Critical Impact of Impending Retirements on Community College Leadership.* Washington, D.C.: American Association of Community Colleges, 2001.

Vaughan, G. B. *Balancing the Presidential Seesaw: Case Studies in Community College Leadership.* Washington, D.C.: American Association of Community Colleges, 2000.

Vaughan, G. B. *Developing Community College Leaders for the Future: Crisis or Opportunity.* Unpublished manuscript, North Carolina State University at Raleigh, 2001. (ED 457 873).

Wubbels, T. "Burn-Out Among Israeli Arab School Principals as a Function of Professional Identity and Interpersonal Relationships with Teachers." *International Journal of Leadership in Education,* 2002, 5(2), 91–105.

Relevant Web Sites

Academic Senate for California Community Colleges: http://www.academicsenate.cc.ca.us.

American Association of Community Colleges' Presidents Academy: The Future Leaders Institute: http://www.aacc.nche.edu ("News & Events" links to the Future Leaders Institute).

American Association of Community Colleges' Leadership Programs for Community College Administrators: http://199.75.76.22/leadership/leadership.asp.

Community College League of California: http://www.ccleague.org.

League for Innovation in the Community College's Executive Leadership Institute: http://www.league.org/league/about/leadinit.htm.

Maricopa Community Colleges' National Community College Chair Academy: http://www.mc.maricopa.edu/other/chair/index.html.

North Texas Community College Consortium: http://www.unt.edu/ntccc.

University of Texas at Austin's Community College Leadership Program: http://www.utexas.edu/academic/cclp.

Virginia Community College System's leadership programs: http://www.so.cc.va.us.

Wo Learning Champions: http://www.wlc.hawaii.edu.

JOANNE E. COOPER *is professor of educational administration, University of Hawaii at Manoa.*

LOUISE PAGOTTO *is assistant dean of arts and sciences, Kapi'olani Community College, Honolulu.*

4

With administrative roles come many changes for faculty leaders, including the perceptions of others, the perception of self, and the skills necessary to remain credible.

Learning on the Job: Moving from Faculty to Administration

Chris McCarthy

I have been chained to the desk lately, working through piles of paper and conducting back-to-back meetings, while students stream by outside my window and memorable teaching takes place within a stone's throw of my office. I work as president of a community college in California, which is a tremendously satisfying job, but there are times when I am taken aback by the contrast between the realities of administrative work and the perception of it by those outside college management ranks. I also realize how little I was prepared for the administrative life, and, as I was moving from faculty through a succession of administrative positions, how few formal opportunities there were for training.

In this chapter, I offer one perspective on the journey from faculty to college president. In it, I detail the positions I held and the kinds of challenges where I had little experience or training for which to prepare. This chapter presumes a point that, as a former teacher of literature, I am drawn to intuitively: in the specific life we find universal truths.

Faculty Member

I chose to leave the faculty after more than a decade of teaching for the "dark side" of administration, as some fellow teachers termed it. I loved the classroom, and some people puzzled over my decision. People who venture into administration are often suspect: I have known many who hungered for an administrative title for a variety of reasons that ranged from the fairly noble (wanting to effect change on a broad scale) to the personal (a desire for achievement and recognition) to the questionable (increasing retirement pay, controlling others, a belief that they know the one true way things should be managed). It was an eagerness for change that primarily spurred me, although in my heart of hearts I am sure that the recognition that comes with advancement played a role.

However, the reality of administrative life was not something I was prepared for, and I found little relevant or accessible training available for those who find themselves thrown into the complex world of academic management. As I talk with other administrators, I realize that I am not alone. For those who have come out of the faculty ranks where, presumably, they were respected and attuned to the work, an ambivalence often surfaces in conversation. They find the rewards of administration counterbalanced in large measure by frustration. They are called on to make decisions based on scant information, without the training that would build decision-making skills. They are expected to enforce accountability in an atmosphere where union contracts and tenure make it nearly impossible to perform anything but the most cursory disciplinary actions. Poets are expected to be budget managers; pianists are expected to become strategic planners.

People respond in different ways. Some return to teaching. Some move from administrative job to administrative job, buying time and energy with each new location. Some retreat into the confines of the office and become swallowed in the paperwork and routine. Others seem to adapt, buoyed by optimism and energy and blessed with interpersonal skills that overcome a lack of training.

I discovered teaching when I received a fellowship in graduate school that paid my tuition. I loved it, and I hoped to live out my life balancing writing, teaching, and travel. I landed in the community college by luck and good fortune. As an English teacher, I taught my classes and worked on various programs that spurred my interest and need for change. I helped develop an honors program, and I taught with a semester abroad. I wrote grants aimed at curriculum development. I was between projects when the division chairmanship, the first stepping-stone to administration, opened. I reasoned that I could try it for a few years, and if things went badly, I could always go back to teaching full time.

Division Chair

My life changed immediately after being elected. Although it was a faculty position, the nature of the job became clear when the vice president told me one morning, "Your job is to represent the administration to the faculty." That afternoon, at a division meeting, the faculty told me, "Your job is to represent the faculty to the administration." My memories of the chairmanship are of being caught in that demilitarized zone where one steps carefully with every move.

My days were full of student complaints, lights that did not work, falling ceiling tiles, ants in offices, faculty concerns, and endless meetings. The building I worked in was falling apart. I pictured myself wearing a tool belt and bandoleer, carrying screwdrivers, chalk, add slips, bug spray, lightbulbs, and extra-strength aspirin. My office was across from the rest rooms, which overflowed on a regular basis. We were cutting budgets, and I sometimes saw myself as an agent of doom, telling students about canceled classes and phoning adjunct faculty to tell them that their jobs no longer existed.

Some of the faculty were wonderful: inspiring, devoted people whose teaching could be compared with anyone's at any university. However, I had no preparation for dealing with the flaws and frailties of people who had taught the same subjects, over and over, for up to forty years, often using lecture notes so old that the folds in their handwritten pages had to be taped. Some absolutely refused to update their teaching materials. One teacher refused to use a copy machine, and an old duplicating machine was kept in a storeroom for his ditto masters. One teacher insisted on using an obscure out-of-print novel in class. She gave her only copy to a student and expected him to read it in two nights and hand it to another, who would do the same until the entire class had read the novel.

Others could stun with an unintended lack of sensitivity. Once, after I was asked to play guitar at the funeral of a colleague, a faculty member approached me, earnest with good intentions, and said, "I want to thank you for playing music at the service. Especially when so many people with so much *more* talent did *nothing*." On another occasion, the same faculty member asked if I was going to the Great Teachers Seminar. Deadpan, I told her I had not been invited but that I was eligible for the Mediocre Teachers Seminar. She was taken aback for a second, then looked me straight in the eye and responded in a tone one might use with a child, "Well, that's good, too."

In any group of people who work in close quarters for many years, slights fester over time, jealousies emerge, and battle lines are drawn over issues as mundane as textbook selection. In one shared office, two warring faculty put a line of masking tape down the center of the room over which the other could not tread. The line stayed there for years. When two other battling teachers passed in the hall, one would routinely turn away, face the wall, and sing loudly to avoid having to speak to her enemy.

Other faculty become ill, physically or emotionally, over time. One adjunct composition teacher moved his class to a room with a stage so he could sing Walt Disney songs and dance during class. He accused his students of being spies planted in class by the mayor. He believed he was in love with newsperson Connie Chung. When he was not rehired, he ordered dozens of hard-core pornographic magazine subscriptions in the names of various administrators delivered to the college mail room. This created a small flurry of campus comment.

I had little training for dealing with the psychological complexity of the group under my supervision. I had little recourse to solve problems caused by a lack of funds, an antiquated building, and resistant elder faculty.

The instance that became a humorous metaphor for my chairmanship occurred when I entered my office, shortly after the rest rooms had overflowed once again, to find a group of custodians installing a metal plate, which was four feet long and wide, on the wall above my desk. Centered on the plate was a large round red light, like those on top of a police car. They told me that when the toilets overflowed, the red light would flash and a siren would sound. I was to call the maintenance crew each time it happened.

Still, good teaching took place, students learned, and lives were changed. The chairmanship felt comfortable over time, and even in a college with no money and with deteriorating facilities, there was a feeling of purpose and challenge. There were personal satisfactions, too. I was able to hire a man who had been my professor in college and who had influenced my decision to study English. His college had closed, and in a strange twist of fate, I now supervised him. It made me feel that life had come full circle. The division came to feel like family, and I enjoyed the job.

In retrospect, it was probably the most important job in my career in terms of learning administrative skills. The division chair's office is the first place problems are taken, and everything from accusations of sexual misconduct to course complaints to faculty conflicts are heard there. It is where training is desperately needed. Since that time, the Chair Academy in Arizona has initiated a yearly conference aimed at entry-level management issues. However, I was unaware of any options other than pursuing a doctorate in education, which is what I decided to do.

I enrolled in a doctoral program at a large, traditional university and found that most of the curriculum centered on doing educational research. I had to seek out faculty who would recognize me as a midcareer professional who wanted course work that was relevant to my daily experience. Although I found the faculty I needed, and I feel that graduate study provided an invaluable experience as well as the "union card" of a doctorate, the institution was not geared at that time to accommodating working professionals. Things have changed, and many schools now offer programs aimed at educators; however, they are expensive, they require a commitment of time, and they do not offer individual opportunities for development for people who cannot commit to the entire program.

When a position as dean came up, I applied and got the job. The evening before I was to take office, I got a call from an irate student who had a complaint about an instructor. The complaint sounded unfounded, and the more the student yelled into the phone, the less rational he became. Finally, realizing that I was not going to satisfy him, he screamed, "Tomorrow, I'm going to the dean."

It was one of those moments we wait for. I replied, "Tomorrow, I am the dean."

Dean of Academic Affairs

My first meeting as dean was with a faculty member who played a leading role in the union. "We should not take teachers out of the classroom for these jobs," he said. "I mean, anyone can do them." He said that he no longer trusted me; if I was the kind of person who would leave the faculty for administration, he had misjudged me for years. This is a common occurrence for faculty who go into administration and one that is always jarring. Years of credibility can be forgotten overnight when we assume the title of dean.

It took some time to make the mental transition from being a faculty chair to an administrator. I was used to the freedom of the faculty to debate, and I did not realize at first that my opinions were no longer completely my own: my function was to support the administrative team. This became clear after a meeting when my supervisor came into my office and closed the door. "You need to decide whether you are faculty or administration," she said.

The lessons of management came quickly but sometimes painfully, and I regretted again that there was no mechanism to guide new administrators as they work through the complex process of managing people. I learned to try and remain reasonable with unreasonable people. I learned to hold heated memos for a day before deciding to send them; in almost every case, they needed softening and greater diplomacy, and the wait afforded that opportunity. I learned to put nothing in writing that could come back to haunt me. I learned that everyone watches what you do and say. An offhand comment, a sly aside, a gossipy quip, or a critical remark will be all over campus. After a few missteps, I learned to be circumspect.

The college was small enough that deans had a variety of responsibilities. I pasted up the schedule of classes on my desk. I worked with the chairs on hiring and personnel issues. I was taken aback that so much time was spent consulting with attorneys on legal issues: I spent three years documenting a faculty member who amassed over one hundred student and faculty complaints. She reported colleagues to every authority she could find: the Equal Employment Opportunity Commission, the Los Angeles Police Department, the Board of Registered Nursing, and Consumer Affairs; we testified in the Civil Court and the Superior Court as she filed vexatious lawsuits. I spent days in depositions and settlement meetings. The teacher remained at the college, although everyone who worked to discipline her eventually left their positions. It was a lesson in the power and permanency of the faculty and the murky nature of our legal climate.

At this point, I was finishing the course work for a doctorate in education, and I realized that law school might have been a more appropriate choice. One of my professors, a former chancellor, said to me one day, "Your main job is to know the law and follow it."

I labored into the evenings and, typically, on Saturdays. I watched faculty finish their classes by noon, and I stared out at empty parking lots after lunch. I had little decision-making power: I was a funnel through which issues would pass, and I tried to defuse as many as I could. I bought garage-sale furniture to outfit my office. Most of the time, as low man in a district bureaucracy, I felt insignificant. On one occasion, after I had tried to get a problem with my paycheck fixed, a district manager reinforced that insignificance when he told me, "The District has a lot more important things to worry about than your paycheck."

John Petersen, the former executive director of our regional accrediting commission, told a joke that echoed through my days as dean. It reinforced, in humor, the feelings of the distrust of those who opt for administrative careers. The joke supplied the definition of a dean: "a mouse learning to become a rat."

Executive Vice President of Instructional Services

I went to a new college district to assume a vice presidency. Moving from one college to another—going to a place where you have no history—presents challenges that are both universal and, inevitably, unique.

We often know relatively little about the colleges to which we submit job applications. We make a leap of faith into the unknown, and we pray that we will land safely. The differences between my former and new college districts illustrate the variety of environments in which we work. I went from a large multicollege district to a single-college district. Where my old college had not seen a new building in thirty years, the new college was poised to begin construction of more than one hundred thousand square feet of instructional space. Where the old college had lost nearly half its student population in the preceding decade, the new college had doubled in size. Where the old college had few ties to the community that surrounded it, the new college was vitally connected to town politics and was strongly influenced by local personalities.

Where my old office had been marked by peeling paint and the garage-sale furniture, the new office was wood paneled and lined with restored photographs that documented the college's history. When I sat at my new desk, I stared across the office at a wall-sized aerial photograph of the college in the 1930s. I was surrounded by black and white photos of students in crew cuts and ties. The pictures were permanently attached to the walls. The message was clear: people may come and go, but the office would be forever.

My previous college sat amid empty parking lots and was surrounded by one of the lowest-income areas in the state. The new college could park only a fraction of the students and was in the midst of a wealthy area. Faculty often moved from one institution to another in the former district. The new college regarded itself as a family, and once people arrived, as the president would say, they would only leave "feet first."

Where my old campus prided itself on reaching out to the remedial population, the new college maintained a strong identity as a transfer institution. My old campus saw its community turn increasingly Hispanic. My new campus saw its community turn increasingly Armenian. On my old campus, I looked for opportunities for creative change. On the new campus, the initial message was clear: things work well here. Don't rock the boat. These differences signaled a completely different culture in which former assumptions about the primary values of the institution might not hold true.

The memory of my first months on the job involves a blur of faces coming at me, asking for immediate decisions on issues I only half understood. Some were outside my experience, such as planning new facilities and dealing with technology issues. Others were complex human problems, and I had little time to delve into them and understand them fully. I did my best to make decisions and move on. I found the institution immensely forgiving.

I learned a few good lessons in the first years on the job. The most important was not to give up the approach and personality that got me there, despite the pressure to do so. Some members of the faculty wanted me to walk in as "a tough guy" and straighten out the problems that they felt were impeding the institution. I became acutely aware of the thin line we walk between control and collegiality, authoritarianism and inclusion as we attempt to be participatory but are saddled with responsibility. I found that each time I operated in opposition to my instincts—bending to someone else's agenda—I got into trouble and regretted my action.

I also realized the solitary nature of the job. It is prudent to keep a little distance, to avoid charges of favoritism and to avoid situations where a disciplinary action might have to be imposed on a friend. I also grew suspicious over time of people's motivations after receiving a few doses of false praise and insincere compliments.

Again, guidance on leadership issues would have been helpful. Instead, like most other administrators, I learned on the job and relied on the advice of a few close colleagues who had held similar positions. I found myself having to accept ambiguity, deal with uncertainty, and expect a lack of resolution on many issues. I learned to accept that someone is probably always angry about something.

I came to understand that every visitor thinks his or her problem is the most important thing you are dealing with. I gradually accepted that you must walk away from some battles, and after you walk away, you have to let go. It was helpful to hear that others dealt with the same issues.

Again, I was often consumed in legal matters. Having taken only a single course in education law, I found myself in the position of deciding which issues should be resolved internally and which should be referred to counsel. That my inexperience would expose the college to significant liability was a real concern.

Although local conferences offered workshops designed to assist, it was rare that a session would provide something of real or lasting significance.

I was pleased to find, and participate in, a summer brainstorming session sponsored by the National Council of Instructional Administrators in Breckenridge, Colorado. Key issues facing colleges were discussed and put into a white paper, and the chance to converse with others who shared similar positions was helpful. However, those opportunities were rare.

After six years, I was offered a presidency at a small college in northern California. Like so many others who realize that movement is often a prerequisite to upward promotion, once again I made the leap of faith.

President

As I write this, I have just concluded one year in my current position. I find it the most satisfying work I have done. This position involves new experiences that are very different from those I have known in the past: working directly with trustees, serving as a liaison with the community, and serving as the voice of the college. I have had the opportunity to become involved in the political process, spearheading a $134 million bond campaign for new college facilities. I have had to deal with the effects of an enormous statewide budget shortfall, and as I write this chapter, we are cutting budgets in unprecedented ways. Still, the accumulation of experiences gained over the past years provides a context that I can draw on as I move through my day. And, at the presidential level, I am finding the kind of leadership training opportunities more and more available than in the past.

As a president, I have had to fill four senior management positions this year. The ranks of those who have the experience and the talent for the work are increasingly rare, and we have readvertised numerous times for some positions. The need for affordable and accessible training programs appears particularly important to me as I survey the pool of candidates applying for our jobs.

I polled managers at one point to ask about their needs, and the overwhelming answer that came back was training in the rules and regulations that govern our actions. Whereas the existing conferences offer global kinds of skill-based workshops, each state has specific codes and requirements that should be addressed at the local level. This is what my managers asked for—training in the nuts and bolts that will help keep them out of trouble.

A few programs stand out as particularly helpful. The summer programs offered through the Graduate Department of Education at Harvard University are excellent. Last summer, I participated in the Seminar for New Presidents, and the mix of people ranged from presidents of prestigious East Coast universities to community colleges to tribal colleges. The interplay between participants was invigorating, and the presentation of issues was compelling. I have spoken with many who have attended their programs aimed at midlevel managers, and they offer the highest accolades.

The Vineyard Symposiums, initiated by former heads of two accrediting commissions, provide brief workshops for presidents that offer the opportunity to candidly explore issues that are central to their institutions. Only among a small group of people who have done the same kind of jobs and who are not relying on each other in the day-to-day work world can sensitive issues be discussed without fear of a backlash.

The American Association of Community Colleges also offers a program for presidents and a variety of annual conferences and workshops. The newly formed Community College Leadership Development Initiatives program at Claremont Graduate University, Claremont, California, offers training for teams of college leaders throughout the year. The Chair Academy in Arizona and the National Council of Instructional Administrators, both previously mentioned, offer valuable programs. An outstanding seminar for female faculty and administrators is offered each year at Asilomar in Monterey, California. Conferences aimed at educators who represent diversity have become more prevalent in recent years. These programs signal an increasing awareness that leadership training is essential and that guidance is needed to convince faculty to leave the security of their positions for the world of administration and to prepare them for the realities of that world.

For many like me, the progress of a career was helped by individuals who went out of their way to provide guidance. I was lucky to find mentors who were willing to put in the time that allowed me to make it through the tough spots and who could provide counsel that attuned me to the realities of administrative life. Not everyone will have such good fortune. Providing a more structured and reliable mechanism for training will pay huge dividends in coming years. This will become increasingly important as the world of higher education becomes more complex and a large number of experienced people retire. The better we prepare people for the realities they will face as they move from the faculty ranks into management, the better chance they will have to succeed, and the better our colleges will fare over the coming years.

Conclusion

I recently found a list of axioms I had prepared for a staff development talk to aspiring administrators. Some of these thoughts were alluded to in the chapter, but perhaps they bear repeating. They may seem self-evident; however, it is easy to forget them, which happens more often than I would like:

- Accept ambiguity
- Understand that uncertainty is a certainty
- Expect a lack of resolution on most issues
- Accept that resolving conflicts is 90 percent of the job
- Accept blame; don't become defensive
- Don't embarrass people publicly
- Accept that someone will often be angry at you
- Expect the unexpected

- Accept that no day will go the way you planned it
- Be reasonable when you are tempted to be unreasonable
- Wait twenty-four hours before sending a strongly worded memo
- Accept that the job can be lonely
- Don't take things personally
- Understand that people expect you to drop everything else to deal with their problems
- Realize you will often have to make decisions about things with which you are woefully lacking in information
- Accept that learning on the job is the normal course of events
- Remember that communication is central to success
- Accept that you must walk away from some battles
- After you walk away, let go
- Say yes whenever you can, but say no when you have to
- Get out of the office regularly and walk the campus
- Be prepared to speak without preparation
- Respond when people call or write, even if you don't have an immediate answer to their problem
- Respect the college traditions and culture
- Realize that everybody is always watching
- Force yourself to take time off
- Remember that people are hungry for validation
- Laugh at yourself

If I were to design a seminar about the realities of the administrative life, those are many of the concepts I would address. They identify the mental attitudes that allow one to bear up under the stress of the job. They speak to the emotional strategies that are central to avoiding feeling overwhelmed by the constant crush of issues and problems. They deal with the affective: the realm of emotions and values that are not often talked about in higher education.

The satisfactions of educational leadership are linked in many ways to the unpredictability of the enterprise. The stories that fill each educator's career may be as varied and colorful as are found in fiction. The achievements that are most satisfying are usually those that are born in crisis, and through the successful exercise of leadership, we find a sense of purpose and meaning in the work.

Although in this chapter I comment on the need for training opportunities that can prepare potential leaders for the unpredictability of an administrative career, I wrote with the understanding that we manage human organizations, and that when we deal with people, the complexity of emotional and interpersonal problems that can affect the institution is unlimited.

There may be no road map that can guide us unscathed through the unexpected detours that are part of each career. Still, by sharing stories and struggles and strategies, by creating opportunities for new administrators to understand that we all deal with common problems, we can assist each other in our development. At the heart of the matter is that it is fascinating work, and we owe those who come into the administrative world, in particular those coming from the culture of faculty, the tools and perspectives that will allow them to find satisfaction and meaning.

CHRIS MCCARTHY *is president-superintendent of Napa Valley College, Napa, California.*

5

*Preparing the next generation of community college
presidents is a responsibility shared by many. A largely
untapped source is the president-board team, which has
primary responsibility for campus-based presidential
leadership development programs.*

Leadership Development: The Role of the President-Board Team

George B. Vaughan, Iris M. Weisman

With the chartering of Harvard University in 1636, the pattern that has dominated American higher education from that day forward was set. Colleges in what would become the United States would have a president who would be responsible to a lay governing board. These two entities—the president and the lay governing board—have played the major roles in charting the direction, mission, role, scope, and destiny of colleges and universities in the United States throughout the nation's history.

The nation's community colleges adopted and adapted the lay board-president model. Reporting to these governing boards are presidents who serve as the professional in charge of the daily, weekly, and yearly operations of the nation's community colleges.

One of the problems facing the community college presidency is that presidents are part of that passing parade that marches forever forward. Indeed, despite what some of those in the position seem to think, community college presidents are not presidents for life. Presidents retire, die, get fired, or move on. For example, 79 percent of presidents surveyed in a 2001 study ($n = 661$) stated that they planned to retire within the next ten years (Weisman and Vaughan, 2002). Another study states that 45 percent ($n = 249$) of the current presidents will retire by 2007 (Shults, 2001). In addition, the average presidential tenure of presidents in 2001 was seven and a half years in their current position and almost nine and a half years in all presidential positions (Weisman and Vaughan, 2002).

So numerous are the anticipated vacancies at the presidential level that the American Association of Community Colleges foretells of an imminent "crisis" that will create a community college leadership gap (Shults, 2001).

Ironically, presidential vacancies themselves—even in large numbers—are not the cause of the leadership gap. The gap is created by a reduction in the number of individuals who are prepared for the presidency (American Association of Community Colleges, 2002) and the number of individuals who actually apply for presidential positions (Evelyn, 2001).

So who has the primary responsibility of preparing future community college presidents for that position? Leadership development cannot and should not exist in isolation, and various opportunities provide the pieces that make up the leadership model: formal graduate education, programs offered through professional associations, and campus-based leadership development programs offered by community colleges. All of these avenues to leadership development are important because the presidency is a complex position, and no one mechanism can address all professional development needs.

Our primary purpose in this chapter is to offer another perspective on the design of leadership development programs that prepare leaders for the presidency. It is important to distinguish between programs that focus on preparing individuals for the presidency from programs that focus on community college leadership in general. Presidential leadership development programs should emphasize those skills, abilities, and knowledge that are unique to the presidency. These skills, abilities, and knowledge must at the same time be broader and more specialized than those often found in a more traditional leadership program. Much of the knowledge and many of the skills and abilities can be gained only through on-site experiences and observations.

We propose three critical criteria for a presidential leadership development program. First, the responsibility for the development of future leaders must be shared by the president and the governing board. Second, the selection of participants in a presidential leadership development program should be limited to "serious, aspiring applicants" (Barwick, 2002, p. 8). A worthwhile presidential leadership development program will require an investment of the institution's financial and human resources; this investment should be made on behalf of only those individuals who are truly passionate about attaining a presidency. Third, a leadership development program specifically aimed at preparing the next generation of community college presidents should focus on providing a comprehensive learning experience over a substantial period.

Responding to the Leadership "Crisis"

Partnerships have been recommended as one approach to designing and delivering leadership development programs (McClenney, 2001). These partnerships are envisioned to be among community colleges, professional associations, and universities and to capitalize on the strength of the various partners to bring a comprehensive approach to leadership development (see Chapter Ten for examples of partnerships). However, a crucial partnership—and one that has the strongest bond and commitment to the welfare of community colleges—has been neglected in leadership development programs: the president-board partnership.

All campus-based leadership development programs must have the approval of the president and the governing board. Indeed, the American Association of Community Colleges (McClenney, 2001) and the Association of Community College Trustees (Polonio, 2002) encourage presidents and trustees to support leadership development programs. Mere support of a leadership development program, however, is insufficient.

Jeff Hockaday, a national consultant who has conducted presidential leadership seminars in ten states and for as many as sixty colleges and fifteen hundred participants, believes strongly that presidents and trustees have *the* responsibility for identifying, cultivating, and educating future leaders. According to Hockaday (oral communication, Aug. 2002), "What we need to do—presidents and boards—is to understand fully that a major piece of our obligation to our college and to the field is to cultivate and shape leaders. If this way of thinking is acceptable to trustees and presidents, then leadership development is *clearly* a local initiative." If we agree with Hockaday, then it is up to current presidents and trustees to see that qualified individuals are available to fill the vacancies as they occur.

Neglected Partnership: The President-Board Team

The team of trustees and president is formidable in terms of power, prestige, influence, and importance. Much of the focus of presidents and boards is placed on the separation between their respective roles: boards make policy, and presidents implement policy. The attention to role differentiation gives a skewed perspective of the actual functioning of and interaction between presidents and their boards. On many undertakings, the president and the board must work as a team if the college is to operate efficiently and successfully. Together, the team leads in establishing, refining, interpreting, and communicating the college's mission; the team sets student tuition (although today state legislators play an increasingly important role in this area); obtains resources; and approves programs, appointments, and expenditures.

Although trustees technically and legally select presidents, they do so from a select pool of applicants. To a large extent, community college presidents decide who goes into the pool (Vaughan, 1998). Does it not make good sense, then, for trustees and presidents to work together to train and develop future presidents?

Setting the Stage: Campus-Based Leadership Development

If campus-based leadership development programs were simple, cost free, and self-administered, there would likely be one at every community college in the country. Unfortunately, they are not: campus-based leadership development programs are complex, and they require human and financial resources to develop and implement. Nonetheless, campus-based programs provide unique learning opportunities that are difficult to replicate in other contexts.

Campus-based leadership development programs, particularly the one proposed in this chapter, are based on the notion of situated cognition. "If we are to learn, we must become embedded in the culture in which the knowing and learning have meaning: conceptual frameworks cannot be meaningfully removed from their settings or practitioners" (Wilson, 1993, p. 77). Leadership development is understood as a situated educational endeavor, with clearly defined learning objectives and structured learning experiences set in the context of an authentic community college environment. Participants in the program experience the real world of the community college presidency and are expected to integrate their individual knowledge, skills, and values with the contextual factors of the situation.

Only through a president-board partnership can a leadership development program provide participants with exposure to all aspects of the community college presidency. Of course, not all facets would be—and should be—included in such a program. Together, the president and board must judiciously identify appropriate situations and contexts for leadership development. Legal and ethical considerations must always be given priority over the opportunity for participants to experience a "presidential moment." Neglecting to do so would be irresponsible on the part of the president and board.

In addition to what to include, *whom* to include must also be carefully considered. The leadership development program must not put the institution at risk of charges of reproducing the current leadership through a narrow set of selection criteria for program participants, limiting promotional opportunities to only those who are included in the program, or stacking the deck against outside candidates when the presidential position becomes vacant.

These considerations are not minor, and they require the president and board to pay careful attention to all aspects of the program design. Yet, the benefits to the organization and the field far outweigh the challenges of launching a campus-based leadership development program.

Selecting the Participants

Two basic questions need to be answered when selecting individuals for a presidential leadership development program: who? and how many?

Who Should Be Selected? A multitude of qualifications could be associated with eligibility for participation in a presidential leadership development program. The president and trustees might consider the applicants' work and educational accomplishments, their prior leadership development experiences, a written statement of their professional goals, and recommendations by applicants' supervisors and peers.

Career Paths. Knowing something about the career paths of current presidents might provide some insight into potential candidates for a presidential leadership development program. What career pathway do most presidents follow before assuming the presidency? Most assuredly, the simple answer is "from somewhere within community colleges," giving lie to the myth that trustees are turning to business and industry, the military, or elsewhere for their presidents. According to a 2001 study, almost 90 percent of the presidents came from within the community college ranks (Weisman and Vaughan, 2002). Over 55 percent of the presidents responding to the 2001 survey reported that they were responsible for their institution's academic program (vice president for academic affairs and so on) before assuming their first presidency. In addition, over 33 percent of the presidents responding to the 2001 survey stated that they were internal candidates when they obtained their first presidency. Furthermore, in 2001 over one-fourth of the current presidents moved into their current position from another community college presidency (Weisman and Vaughan, 2002).

The odds are, then, that the successful applicant will already be employed in a community college, serving as the college's chief academic officer or as a president at another community college. Moreover, there is one chance in three that the person will be currently employed at the institution at which he or she assumes the presidency. It stands to reason, therefore, that the team should select the presidential leadership development program participants from within the community college ranks.

Professional Commitment. There is one qualification that is essential and irrefutable for participation in a presidential leadership development program: true commitment to the presidency.

The presidency requires more than a passion for the glitz and glamour of a powerful position. Being a successful president requires a commitment to the mission of the community college and a vision of the presidency as a personal and professional goal, as opposed to a "next step in a career path" (Barwick, 2002).

Commitment to Diversity. Ultimately, trustees select the president who best "fits" their institution (Barwick, 2002). "Fit" and replication are not synonymous, and we caution against assuming that institutional fit can be achieved only by selecting candidates who mirror the characteristics of the individuals doing the selection. Why is the selection of sameness a concern? A brief profile of current presidents and trustees provides the answer. In 2001, almost 86 percent of the nation's community college presidents were white; 6.4 percent were African American; 5.5 percent were Hispanic; the remainder came from Native American, Asian, and other ethnic and racial groups. The percentage of minority presidents increased from 11 percent in 1996 to 14 percent in 2001. The percentage of women community college presidents rose from 11 percent in 1991 to 28 percent by 2001 (Weisman and Vaughan, 2002).

Of the sixty-five hundred or so men and women who served on the governing boards of the nation's community colleges in 1995, more than 86 percent were white, 7.9 percent were African American, and 2.3 percent were Hispanic (Vaughan and Weisman, 1997). As is the case with the percentage of minority and female presidents, women fare much better than minorities in governing board membership. In 1995, women made up 33 percent of the community college trustees (Vaughan and Weisman, 1997).

Although the number of women and people of ethnic and racial minority groups has increased within the ranks of the presidency and on boards, adequate representation has still not been achieved. Therefore, as the president-board team selects individuals for presidential leadership development programs, the needs of the profession to increase diversity among the pool of future presidents must be considered.

A word of caution: "Sameness" or replication can also be represented in a person's education, career path, and community activities. Presidents and trustees are encouraged to take a broad perspective on how one can demonstrate the potential for presidential leadership and to avoid a narrow checklist of selection criteria. There is a vast pool of individuals—women and minorities, as well as white—on the nation's community college campuses just waiting to be invited to sit at the leadership table. It behooves trustees and presidents, knowing that a vast number of presidential vacancies will occur, to have well-qualified replacements waiting in the wings.

How Many Should Be Selected? Unlike a general leadership development program that might be compared with a broad, introductory undergraduate course with thirty or more students and one instructor, a presidential leadership development program is more similar to a graduate—or postgraduate—seminar, in which a handful of students participate in focused, intense study. We recommend that the number of individuals participating in a campus-based presidential leadership development program be limited to two or three at any one time.

Investing in the Future Benefits the College

Campus-based leadership development programs, both those created for potential leaders throughout the organization and those created specifically for aspiring presidents, tend to be relatively short, lasting anywhere from a few days to a year. The presidential leadership development program conceptualized in this chapter is a deeper, more comprehensive program than most existing programs. Similar to Macomb County Community College's Janus Program in Warren, Michigan (Lorenzo and DeMarte, 2002), the model presented here involves the infusion of the program participants into a wide variety of decision-making and policymaking activities. Program participants are immersed in academic, student services, fiscal, and administrative responsibilities and the governance of the college. They are exposed to the full flavor of the presidency.

Preparing leaders for the future is perhaps not sufficient reason to convince the president and trustees team to commit itself to a campus-based leadership program. What, then, are the other benefits that may accrue to the college itself from the program?

Participants' deepened understanding of and commitment to the college represent important benefits to the college that can pay off in any number of ways. For example, participants might serve as ambassadors of the college in the community and at professional meetings.

Trustees and the president can affirm their commitment to diversity by identifying, cultivating, and educating members of underrepresented groups through the presidential leadership development program. If many colleges establish such programs, they can take major steps toward closing the gap that currently exists between the percentages of white and minority presidents and of male and female presidents.

The board will learn much by creating a meaningful and successful presidential leadership development program. Then, should a presidential vacancy occur, the trustees will be well versed in developing an informed and reasoned position description for the new president. They will also be able to ask questions to which they want and expect candidates for the presidency to provide sound answers.

Presidents will find that by sharing their knowledge, they will sharpen their own skills and knowledge. No president wants to appear ill informed or ill prepared when he or she is instructing a member of the college community on leadership skills. And the presidential leadership development program will require that the president be engaged in constant teaching, the activity that goes to the heart of the enterprise. The same applies to other members of the college's administrative team.

Another major benefit will be that, with each cycle of the program, the college has prepared two or three individuals for leadership positions in the community college. If the leadership development program is successful, eventually one of the participants will be sitting in a president's chair, perhaps the one at the college that has honed his or her leadership skills. One would hope that that person, too, would see the value of leadership development and carry on the tradition of helping others achieve their potential as leaders.

Presidential Leadership Development Proposal

Following are initial recommendations on developing a campus-based presidential leadership development program.

Establishment of the Presidential-Board Partnership. To begin the process of leadership development on campus, the trustees and the president must commit to leadership development and view that development as a priority and as a local undertaking. The president must be willing to involve trustees in developing leaders to a degree that may cross the traditional (and often imaginary) line that separates policymaking from administration. Then, the president-trustee team can begin the process of leadership development on their campus. The following are some steps that can be taken in formulating an effective process.

The president must provide trustees with a clear profile of current presidents, what career paths they follow, and other characteristics. This information will assist trustees in identifying future leaders. For example, if trustees know that 90 percent of the current presidents come from within the community college field, they will obviously consider current college employees as a possible source of future presidents. The president's role in providing trustees with information is critical because almost 93 percent of the trustees responding to one survey said that they rely on the president or the president's staff for the information they receive about the college (Vaughan and Weisman, 1997).

Once armed with adequate information, the president and trustees should carefully examine the qualifications and skills they seek in an effective leader. This examination should result in a list of personal attributes (for example, integrity) and skills and abilities (for example, communicates effectively) that they view as essential for an effective leader. The president and board chair should issue a statement to the college community announcing their commitment to leadership development and giving some indication of how the process will unfold.

Participant Selection. The president and staff should identify a number of individuals within the college ranks who have an interest in and the potential for leadership at the presidential level. Faculty members should not be ignored in this part of the process because many teaching faculty members have the skills and attributes to be effective leaders. What they often lack is an avenue for breaking into the administrative ranks.

Trustees tend to select a new president (and, thus, participants) who is much like the current one if the current president is well liked. If the current president is unpopular, trustees may well look for someone who appears to be just the opposite of the current president. Neither approach is acceptable when selecting participants for the leadership development program, for Kerr and Gade (1986) are correct in their observation that there is "no such thing as the presidential type." Trustees and the president should avoid selecting only those individuals who look, think, and act like the current president. Trustees can avoid the "cloning syndrome" if they work with the president to develop a position description for participants of the leadership development program based on skills, experience, commitment, and demands of the presidency, rather than considering only personalities (although personalities can be important to effective leadership) and appearances.

Participants should be exposed to leadership concepts and theory as quickly and as effectively as possible. Consultants should work with the group for several days to give members of the group a better idea of what presidential leadership entails. Ideally, the president and a member of the governing board should sit through all or much of the workshop.

Once the group has participated in the workshop, the president submits the names and resumés to the governing board, and the president and staff share what they know about the individuals with members of the board. After the board becomes familiar with the individuals, a series of interviews is scheduled with the board and president. Two or three of these individuals will be selected to participate in the college's newly formed presidential leadership development program. Those selected should be given some reduction in duties for the duration of the leadership development program.

Comprehensive Presidential Leadership Development Program. The proof of the pudding is indeed in the eating when it comes to leadership development. Presidents are busy, trustees are busy, and those individuals selected to participate in the leadership development program will be busy. It makes sense, then, to build leadership development into the daily activities of those individuals involved with and selected to participate in the college's leadership development program. Indeed, what better laboratory for leadership development than the college itself? The following suggestions might help get the program off the ground.

Plan the program for a two-year period. This time frame will help ensure that the participants get a thorough introduction into the nuances and intricacies of leadership. The two-year period will also permit the participants to get in-depth experience in a number of areas. Trustees, and especially presidents, must realize early that the program is more than a mentoring program whereby each participant visits with a mentor once a month or so. The few participants must receive the attention they require and deserve.

Each segment of the college should develop a plan through which participants in the presidential leadership development program can get "hands-on" experience. For example, most individuals on campus have limited or no experience in planning a budget and have little understanding of the admissions process. The individuals in the program must be involved in the decisions that affect each administrative unit about which they are learning.

The board should invite participants to work actively with the board. Most individuals below the vice president level have little idea of how a board functions or why it makes the decisions it makes. New presidents who suddenly find themselves working closely with a board often have little idea of how to act or what to do. To educate participants fully about board activities, the board should include attendance at committee meetings as well as board meetings. Occasionally participants should be asked questions regarding critical issues. This interaction will give participants a good idea of what the board does and will give the board an opportunity to observe how future leaders think and act.

The president should include participants in staff meetings when appropriate. As with the trustees, the president should ask participants questions and evaluate their answers. These activities will provide the president with a firsthand view of how participants think and act.

The above are just a beginning point for activities that could be planned for participants in a college's leadership development program. Each president-trustee team will have its own agenda and its own idea of activities that enhance leadership. In some cases, the locally developed program might be supplemented by work on fundamental leadership issues such as organizational development, ethics, and regional or national community college issues. Linkages might be formed with seminars or other convenient activities that would complement the program at the college.

Concluding Remarks

In the above discussion, we recommend that trustees and presidents become actively engaged in leadership development on their own campuses. The stage is set; all that is required is commitment and action. For trustees and presidents to continue to ignore the need for planned leadership development is to shirk a crucial responsibility of senior leaders. To act now is to act with vision because the vacancies at the presidential level will occur, and they will be filled. Who fills them is the responsibility of current board members and current presidents.

References

American Association of Community Colleges (AACC). *Leadership 2020: Recruitment, Preparation, and Support,* 2002. [http://www.aacc.nche.edu/Content/ContentGroups/Leadership_Programs1/Leadership_2020.htm]. Accessed Sept. 8, 2002.

Barwick, J. "Leadership Development: Same Trail, New Vistas." *Community College Journal,* Aug./Sept. 2002, *73,* 6–11.

Evelyn, J. "Community Colleges Face a Crisis of Leadership." *Chronicle of Higher Education,* Apr. 6, 2001, p. A36.

Kerr, C., and Gade, M. L. *The Many Lives of Academic Presidents: Time, Place, and Character.* Washington, D.C.: Association of Governing Boards, 1986.

Lorenzo, A. L., and DeMarte, D. T. "Recruiting and Developing Leaders for the 21st Century." In D. F. Campbell (ed.), *The Leadership Gap: Model Strategies for Leadership Development.* Washington, D.C.: Community College Press, 2002.

McClenney, K. M. "Converting Crisis to Opportunity: The AACC Community College Leadership Summit." *Community College Journal,* June/July 2001, *71*(6), 24–27.

Polonio, N. "What Can Boards Do to Cultivate the Next Generation of Presidents?" *Trustee Quarterly,* Winter 2002, pp. 22–23, 44.

Sharples, D. K., and Carroll, C. "Beacon Leadership Program," In D. F. Campbell (ed.), *The Leadership Gap: Model Strategies for Leadership Development.* Washington, D.C.: Community College Press, 2002.

Shults, C. *The Critical Impact of Impending Retirements on Community College Leadership.* AACC/Leadership Series Research Brief no. 1. Washington, D.C.: American Association of Community Colleges, 2001.

Vaughan, G. B. "No New Leaders." *Community College Week,* Aug. 24, 1998, pp. 4–5.

Vaughan, G. B., and Weisman, I. M. *Community College Trustees: Leading on Behalf of Their Communities.* Washington, D. C.: Association of Community College Trustees, 1997.

Weisman, I. M., and Vaughan, G. B. *The Community College Presidency 2001.* AACC/Leadership Series Research Brief no. 3. Washington, D.C.: American Association of Community Colleges, 2002.

Wilson, A. "The Promise of Situated Cognition," In S. Merriam (ed.), *An Update on Adult Learning Theory.* San Francisco: Jossey-Bass, 1993.

GEORGE B. VAUGHAN *is professor of higher education at North Carolina State University in Raleigh; before becoming a professor, he served as a community college president for seventeen years.*

IRIS M. WEISMAN *is associate professor of higher education and chair, Community College Management, at Antioch University McGregor, Yellow Springs, Ohio.*

6

University doctoral programs play a significant role in preparing community college leaders. Criteria of successful programs are discussed, along with how they should relate to community college professionals entering the program.

Role of Universities in Leadership Development

Betty Duvall

Community colleges are expected to need new leaders as a wave of retirements will soon swamp these colleges (Shults, 2001). Community college leadership programs culminating in a doctoral degree are increasingly perceived as important when colleges conduct searches for new leaders. About one hundred such programs are inventoried on the American Association of Community Colleges' Web site (http://www.aacc.nche.edu). Some are designed specifically for community colleges, some encompass all of higher education, and others target education leaders generally, with separate tracks for K-12 and community colleges. Programs have begun to feature new delivery methods and new designs in an effort to attract students and to fill the anticipated gap in leader availability.

Early Leadership Preparation

Early in the history of community colleges, leaders and administrators were like the faculty they led. They held master's degrees, usually in a subject area, and that, along with experience gained through moving up the ranks, was deemed sufficient. Leadership positions were filled by those who distinguished themselves as good teachers, were promoted to department chair, then up the administrative ladder. Any leadership training was acquired through on-the-job experience. In the 1950s and 1960s, community colleges grew more complex, and formal study in higher education that led to a doctoral degree emerged as important. Experience remained central; however, the growing emphasis on formal study was influenced, no doubt, by the desire to "professionalize" leadership roles and by the view of education and leadership as an accepted body of knowledge within the academy. This trend was also fueled by the rapid growth of new community colleges and the lack of time to "grow" new leaders from within the institution. Formal degrees or training, once not necessary for higher-level positions, became an expectation.

Assuming that leaders were prepared as leaders simply because they had moved up the ranks posed problems for community colleges. First, community colleges' core mission as comprehensive institutions required leaders who were knowledgeable in many areas. The leader whose preparation was based on the experience of being a teacher, a department chair, instructional dean, and then president often meant that that person lacked knowledge in a number of areas—for example, student support services, instructional technology, noncredit programming—important to the college. No matter what internal career path and related experience one pursued, this alone did not provide the programmatic background needed for the most senior positions.

Furthermore, as the role of the president expanded beyond chief instructional leader, relying only on job experience may not have provided the business skills required (financial management, land and building acquisition, insurance, and the like). Work with legislators and with foundations, lobbying, managing elections for bonds, tax rate and tuition increases, collective bargaining, litigation—all these issues were added to the duties of an individual whose experience was typically centered around teaching and learning. The foundation for these additional skills, however, could be acquired through formal learning, then enhanced through on-the-job experience. With formal education plus learning gained from experience, community college leaders were better prepared for the demands made on them by the colleges they led and by their communities.

One of the major issues surrounding a tradition of seeking leadership from within ranks was the predominance of white men in top leadership positions. Women and people of color were less likely to gain promotion through the ranks, and those in charge naturally looked for replacements who looked like them. Formal degrees were a wedge driven in the access door by women and people of color; degrees helped demonstrate that they were competent leaders ready to assume their rightful role in community college leadership.

Today few people attain the presidency or any other top-level leadership position in community colleges without a terminal degree. The commonly held belief is that most applicants will have a doctoral degree (though, interestingly, most job announcements list this qualification as "desirable" as opposed to "required"). The expectation of experience in positions of increasing responsibility remains, for the most part, unchanged.

Behind the expectation that leaders will hold a doctoral degree, however, is the assumption that this attainment indicates a sound theoretical base that will be of assistance in addressing real problems. Formal study helps leaders in formulating ideas and philosophies and determining methods and actions. In addition, the doctoral degree symbolizes a level of academic attainment with which community colleges—certainly their boards of trustees—wish to associate.

Nature of Doctoral Study

One of the important purposes that may be assigned to community college leadership programs in universities was set out long ago by John Henry Newman (1907) in his essay, "The Idea of a University." Although describing the university as a whole, his goals are relevant to university leadership programs: "It is a place where inquiry is pushed forward, and discoveries verified and perfected, and rashness rendered innocuous, and error exposed, by the collision of mind with mind, and knowledge with knowledge." Surely quality university programs of study encourage students to engage in organized inquiry, to research their field in search of new discoveries, and to examine the veracity of those discoveries. Community college leadership programs recognize that learning is best done in a social community, not just solitary inquiry, and that new learning and being with other new learners lead to new information and to making new meaning of existing information.

Doctoral programs are designed to encourage the student to explore new knowledge and to consider new ideas. Basic to study at this level is the challenge to think in a different way. Modern doctoral work aims to be less about the acquisition of knowledge (although that is an important part of any program) and the ability to restate that knowledge in exams. Instead, it strives to be more about the ability to question, to investigate, to be able to view issues from different perspectives, and to understand and accept the prevalence of ambiguity and paradox.

Furthermore, university leadership programs are a resource to the field through student and faculty research. The inquiry generated at the university can enrich and inform practice within community colleges. This resource can be vital to the colleges, which above all other higher education institutions value change, rapid response to community and learner needs, and improvements in teaching and services.

For most graduate students, obtaining the terminal degree requires a considerable investment in time and money and inconvenience for their family and oftentimes for professional colleagues as well. These factors certainly condition student requirements and expectations.

Community College Practice

Community colleges themselves are, at present, both old and new: "old" in the sense that community colleges as envisioned after World War II have existed for thirty to forty years, and there is a commonly understood and accepted community college mission, purpose, and philosophy. They are at the same time "new" because the community college strength advocated by its proponents is that community colleges continue to evolve and grow within the common mission.

This balance between the old and the new makes special requirements of leaders. If leaders lead only from experience, they tend to be looking back. If on the other hand they lead from new learning, that is, new meaning made from existing knowledge and from new discoveries, they will be encouraged to look forward. Leaders who themselves are comfortable with growth and change will likely want to lead their institutions to grow and change, to be vital and responsive.

Contemporary views of leadership in both administrative and faculty contexts emphasize the notion that truth is found in paradox. Leaders understand that they may be faced with two or more decision options, each different, yet all true. They understand that change is not a matter of choice but a phase in the institution's development and that pressure for change will appear continuously. Making matters even more complex, fundamental ambiguities permeate the lives of leaders. Working in environments where institutional aims are changing (and often unclear), where decision information is inadequate, and where the consequences of a decision are unclear is commonplace.

Leaders who have in important ways come to terms with paradox and ambiguity are in preferred positions to deal with the long and dynamic list of specific issues they will face. At the present time, this list would include the application of technology in teaching and learning, the emphasis on assessing learning outcomes, public concerns for institutional accountability, the management of information (student, employee, financial) within the institution, community relations, raising funds from both public and private sources, media relations, federal and state legal issues, litigation, personnel management, internal constituent relations including governance, collective bargaining, state and local finance issues including facility bonds, facility management, accreditation requirements, and fair treatment of intellectual property. Well-designed doctoral programs will make sure that students receive some exposure to these types of practical issues.

Existing Leader Preparation Programs

The American Association of Community Colleges inventory lists sixteen programs with community college emphasis (perhaps even fewer are singularly designed for community college leaders). Many more programs are listed that are more inclusive and focus on leadership in higher education. A similar list is maintained by the ERIC Clearinghouse for Community Colleges (http://www.gseis. ucla.edu/ERIC/gradprog).

Debra Bragg (2002) notes a number of programs that have concentrated on community college leadership. Many of these programs are distinguished by unique and innovative approaches to instruction, including learning communities, cohorts, internships, and the use of technology. Examining these practices is useful.

A cohort or learning community approach admits students to the program as a group, and that group remains together throughout their formal study. Project (or team) learning is an important component with attention to mutual discovery and sharing. This teamwork practice offers students important experience for their careers. The feeling of connectedness cohorts generate, along with the sharing of current on-the-job issues and experiences, makes this approach especially relevant to practitioners.

Many university leadership programs have rushed to employ technology as a delivery means or as a significant instructional support mechanism. An increasing number of private institutions provide doctoral programs by Internet delivery, hoping to appeal to working students who may be more time and place sensitive than cost sensitive. Other programs use the Internet or other technologies such as two-way compressed interactive video to "commute" to on-campus programs.

Structured internships recognize the practitioner component of community college leadership training. Most graduates of university community college programs have as their goal work as community college administrators. Students may continue to actively pursue scholarly investigation within their own practice, but they do not expect to have a career in research. Instead of numerous research projects, internships allow students to access their learning to date and to supplement and enhance that learning through guided practical experience. Internships also recognize the value of hands-on learning, perhaps, again, a reflection of the community college instructional philosophy and concern for career preparation.

Some programs hold courses on weekends or at times after work that facilitate attendance by working professionals. Still others offer targeted certificate programs for students who do not yet wish to begin a full doctoral program but who want to add to their formal learning.

Universities and related organizations, notably the American Association of Women in Community Colleges, have been active in identifying current skills and qualities found in the ideal leader. Inventories and assessment tools allow students to identify their strengths and needs and to develop study programs designed to fill in any gaps; these can also be used to determine a course of study within a formal leadership program. Many such tools exist, developed by university programs (University of Florida is an example) and by leadership centers and organizations. Inventories of leadership skills can also be used for building the curriculum for formal learning programs.

Responsiveness of University Programs

Such innovation in university gradate programs does not come easily. University leaders and faculty can be reluctant to leave practices that have long histories of serving learners' needs. Faculty rewards are often based on traditional practice. Recognizing that new learners have different needs does not happen quickly in settings where traditional learning is the norm. Although many universities have formally adopted expanded definitions of scholarship beyond the traditional research and publishing as part of their promotion and tenure policy, in fact, the primary path to tenure and full professor remains published research. If teaching is recognized at all, it is as traditional teaching: teacher and students on campus for a fifteen-week session. Developing and delivering nontraditional learning experiences for adult students with professions of their own can be very different. University colleagues accustomed to traditional teaching find it difficult to understand and reward new methods. For example, working community college professionals who are also university students see the break times in the academic calendar as opportunities to work with university professors. But because community colleges and universities share break times (spring break, between terms, and so forth), these are customarily also break times for university faculty; many university faculty members are not accustomed to using these periods for contact with students.

The education discipline generally, and certainly community college doctoral programs in particular, still struggle to gain acceptance as an area of scholarly work. Qualitative research and study of one's own practice—despite progress made in recent years of recognizing them as appropriate to the social sciences—are often still judged as "less than" by university colleagues in the "hard" sciences and by professors who have earned their own rewards through quantitative work.

Future Directions

Some universities have begun to embrace new curricular design and new methods of delivery and to challenge traditional university practice. However, most programs of higher education remain well within the traditional university model. The recent emphasis on the present and coming need for new leaders in community colleges has encouraged entrepreneurial institutions to explore new delivery methods. Currently, prospective students can find programs where all or almost all instruction is delivered online, requiring no attendance on campus. Other programs have been developed that totally move away from the key elements of traditional university models. For example, some programs do away with a dissertation requirement, totally ignoring such a requirement or substituting projects or a far less rigorous terminal experience; in some cases, mentors substitute for faculty.

Although innovation and creativity are to be welcomed—are, in fact, badly needed—the higher education community would be well advised to proceed with caution. First, prospective students want to be sure that they are getting a "real" doctorate, one that will be understood and respected by employers and colleagues. Second, to totally reject all that has worked in formal education programs seems reckless. Far better to develop new models that accommodate needs but also that challenge students in a scholarly way, that prepare them for not only jobs but also the paths their careers are likely to take. Requiring students to think deeply and to explore and develop research will better prepare future leaders to face new challenges. Community colleges have long been charged with a reluctance to examine themselves and to ask the hard questions. Leaders for the future need to be prepared to do just that.

Some university-based community college leadership programs offer suggestions for creating successful programs. For example, community college cohorts and classes should be separate from other education leadership preparation (both K-12 and higher education). A proper emphasis on issues unique to community colleges takes place best when all students have similar career goals. Cohorts developed as learning communities are powerful teaching and learning experiences. Work now and in the future is likely to involve teams; doctoral programs have a responsibility to develop the ability to work in teams. In addition, deliberate attention to developing learning communities conveys an important learning method and enhances students' feelings of belonging and being connected. Many institutions talk about learning communities; few actually deliberately develop them.

Although many successful programs attract a regional population, the learning experience is greatly enriched through bringing as much diversity—in all definitions of diversity—into the program as possible. Involvement of students from other regions and international students from community colleges in other countries should be part of this. An international cohort separate from other cohorts would address the specific needs of international students. Finding ways for cohorts to work together would enhance each group's experience. In addition, technology should be incorporated in programs to allow students to learn in that format, a method likely to be used in the community colleges they lead.

A variety of faculty teaching in community college leadership programs is desirable. Traditional university faculty whose expectations include research is important. At the same time, programs profit from faculty who have been community college practitioners. Although universities are not likely to invest in those who have long years of service (and high salary expectations) but lack a significant record of research and publishing, such leaders bring an important legitimacy and immediacy to learning that is often inspiring. Using short-term appointments such as visiting scholar or research professor can offer the advantage of adding community college leaders while avoiding long-term, expensive appointments.

Part-time faculty can also provide the practical perspective in the classroom. Who better to teach a finance class than a community college vice president for administration? Who better to be a guest lecturer in a law class than an attorney who is practicing law that relates to community college students and faculty? However, programs cannot exist without a core of full-time tenured faculty. Faculty must plan the curriculum and be in sufficient number to advise students through their independent research and writing. Universities cannot rely too heavily on adjunct or honorary appointments to do the core faculty job. Adjunct and honorary faculty can enrich the learning experience but are no substitute for full-time professors with ongoing responsibility for providing a solid academic learning experience.

Many students come to doctoral programs as adult working professionals with considerable responsibility in their own college. In their own institution, they encourage faculty to recognize the needs and learning styles of adult learners. They expect the same for themselves as students. The old pattern of graduate student as willing and devoted assistant to the professor will not work. Successful programs will treat students as the working professionals they are. Programs must address practical problems in a manner reflective of a solid theoretical base. Students look for an immediate return on their investment of time and money. The practical ideas a student can bring back to the workplace become important for both the student and his or her coworkers.

Providing financial assistance to community college leadership students will enlarge the leadership pool. Students may hold full-time jobs and also carry considerable personal financial obligations. Scholarships and stipends available to working and part-time students will aid in bringing new leaders to programs. In addition, the location and scheduling format of the program figure greatly in attracting diverse students and enhancing the likelihood of success. Planned retreats, special seminars, and miniconferences are also important; they provide the necessary isolation for students to engage in reflective inquiry concerning their leadership skill development.

Community college leadership students, regardless of whether the program results in a Ph.D. or an Ed.D, need to learn how to do original research. Community college leaders have a responsibility to give back to their profession in the form of research. They know the questions worthy of investigation; they know where the relevant data are or might be found. Because the definition of scholarship has been broadened and qualitative and action research are accepted practices within the academic community, the time is right for practitioners to be more involved in research. Doctoral programs have a responsibility to prepare leaders to research and report their findings. A mere terminal project or experience is not appropriate to the doctoral experience.

University leadership programs should seek to cooperate with similar programs in other universities. This can bring a richer diversity to the learning experience and also allow each program to develop specialized areas of strength. To this end, interesting examples of articulated and joint doctoral programs have appeared in recent years.

Successful programs will develop and publish expected student learning outcomes. Students should be involved in developing outcomes, and these should be regularly reviewed to provide feedback and improvement. Outcomes might include leaders' roles as lifelong learner, as instructional leader, and as community college leader. Secondary items might include the demonstration of the ability to articulate and promote the unique mission of the community college; establish college policies and procedures that protect faculty, staff, and students' rights and responsibilities; analyze college structure, processes, and policies for their effect on students; collaborate with community agencies, business and industry, and other schools and colleges involved in the education of adult learners; lead using systems analysis of a situation that involves local, state, national, and international perspectives; and promote valuing of cultural pluralism and multicultural education.

Summary

Successful community college leadership programs currently exist in a few universities. Given the need for new community college leaders, such programs are likely to continue to improve and expand. The limited number of programs specializing in community colleges is insufficient to meet the national needs in the field, and more generalized programs are a pale substitute because they do not recognize the uniqueness of community colleges. The most successful programs specialize in community colleges, and they emulate the institutions they serve. Those programs are as innovative, as desirous of change, and as willing to challenge the traditional as the institutions they are designed to serve.

References

American Association of Community Colleges. "Characteristics of Community College Leaders," 2002. [http://www.aacc.nche.edu]. Accessed Sept. 15, 2002.

Bragg, D. "Doing Their Best: Exemplary Graduate Leadership Programs." *Community College Journal*, Aug./Sept. 2002, 77(1), 49–53.

Newman, J. H. *The Idea of a University*. Reprinted 1907. [http://www.newmanreader.org/works/idea]. Accessed June 7, 2003.

Shults, C. *The Critical Impact of Impending Retirements on Community College Leadership*. AACC/Leadership Series Research Brief no.1. Washington, D.C.: American Association of Community Colleges, 2001.

BETTY DUVALL *is professor of higher education and coordinator of the Community College Leadership program at Oregon State University, Corvallis.*

*In this formative evaluation, the author examines a
leadership development program provided by a
professional association and includes implications for
other programs.*

Administration 101: Evaluation of a Professional Development Program

Cristina Chiriboga

Formal graduate education programs and campus-based leadership initiatives meet only part of the need for community college leadership training programs (Barnes and others, 1987; Chancellor's Task Force, 2002). Professional associations may offer additional valuable training opportunities, ones that can be uniquely attuned to regional needs defined by the field itself. One such program is "Administration 101," offered through California's primary professional association for administrators, the Association of California Community College Administrators (ACCCA).

The purpose of the work reported in this chapter was to describe and evaluate the program content, learning activities, and general program organization of Administration 101 as the program activities were developing. Finally, this evaluation was intended to provide the ACCCA program organizers with the information required to make changes, if needed, in the ways that Administration 101 was being offered.

Program Description: Administration 101

In summer 2001, ACCCA conducted the first Administration 101 program at the University of California, Los Angeles. The program was delivered in an intensive five-day format. Administration 101 consisted of a series of presentations focusing on identified curriculum content areas, including

California community college governance: the mission and goals of California
community colleges, community college governmental relations, the role

of the system's board of governors and the governance structure at local levels, and the principle of consultative or participative governance as defined in state law

Instruction and student services: the community college curriculum development process, matriculation and assessment requirements, enrollment management, and selected aspects of unique instructional delivery modes such as distance education and learning support services

Institutional dynamics: research and strategic planning tools for understanding institutional culture and politics, and exploring collaboration, communication, and linkages with the community for purposes of educational and economic development

Human resources: Education Code and requirements for recruitment, selection, hiring, and the tenure process for community college faculty as well as understanding collective bargaining and various legal aspects of human resource management

Finance and budget development: historical overview of funding mechanisms in California, an understanding of general fund and categorical programs (hard versus soft monies), workload measures, critical regulations such as the "50 percent law" that requires prescribed levels of expenditures for direct instructional services, and budget development strategies and key budget management activities

Current issues and challenges, including such critical activities as technology planning, the new accreditation standards developed by the regional accreditation association, and effective student retention program models

Interspersed throughout the program were social events such as group dinners held at popular local restaurants and a free afternoon that allowed for participant networking and leisure time. The program closed with integrative sessions organized around themes of building community (in 2001) and of creating effective student retention models (in 2002).

Originally planned for a maximum of fifty participants in 2001, the program was immediately oversubscribed, and registration had to be limited to sixty-five. Participants were drawn from every region of the state, from every type of institution (single- and multicollege districts) and from every professional level (faculty coordinators and directors through the ranks of deans, vice presidents, and even one new president). Based on this initial response, the ACCCA board resolved to continue Administration 101 and to build on the model. The second session was held in summer 2002 to the same high level of participation.

Administration 101 is best understood as a kind of "first response" to the current need for administrative professional leadership development within the state. Although it is not the only response, the ACCCA program does represent a unique, field-driven approach, one that ACCCA intends to offer on an ongoing basis.

Competencies

According to Townsend and Bassoppo-Moyo (1997), essential professional skills and knowledge needed by college administrators involve contextual, technical, conceptual, and interpersonal communication and integrative and adaptive competencies. Such a classification could be envisioned as a continuum of competencies ranging from managerial to leadership skills, with contextual, technical, and interpersonal communication skills that address what could be classified as administrative managerial tasks, whereas integrative and adaptive skills could be said to focus on broader leadership challenges.

The Administration 101 curriculum was designed to address aspects of all of these. For example, the conceptual framework was addressed by sessions on "mission and governance"; technical dimensions were addressed in components on "human resources," "finance and budget," and "instruction and student services"; interpersonal communication skills were emphasized in sessions dealing with governance and in case studies presented throughout the program; and integrative and adaptive professional competencies were strongly in evidence in the presentations on "student retention" and "accreditation." Contextual competencies were addressed in sessions on "institutional dynamics" and through case studies in instruction and student services. These categories emphasize real-world applications and competencies considered essential for administrators who function in the California community college system. The positive evaluation responses of Administration 101 participants and presenters appeared to validate this system of categories as interpreted and applied by California community college practitioners.

Methods of the Evaluation

This program evaluation merged the perspectives of two populations of working professionals: the program presenters and the program participants. During both summer 2001 and summer 2002 sessions, participants were asked to complete questionnaires rating each of the session presentations for content, presentation format, usefulness, and overall quality. Respondents checked options of "needs improvement," "average," or "excellent" for each measure. In addition, respondents were given the opportunity to write open-ended comments for each session. At the conclusion of the 2001 and 2002 programs, participants also completed a final program evaluation form to assess program strengths and areas for improvement.

The research design of this study focused on program format and delivery and whether delivery strategies could be changed to facilitate participant learning or whether topics or curriculum elements should be eliminated, incorporated, or expanded. In addition to the analysis of the evaluation questionnaires and comments, focus group sessions were held with selected members of the summer 2002 cohort to assess program content and delivery. Follow-up surveys asked all summer 2002 participants to comment on the value and usefulness of Administration 101. Finally, individual phone interviews were conducted with presenters from the first summer session who were returning to present in the second summer session.

Participant Sample. The summer 2001 cohort included thirty-three men and thirty-two women and was composed of representatives drawn from every major ethnic group within the system. The first Administration 101 cohort ranged widely in years of experience, including individuals in their first year of administrative work to those with decades of experience. A few participants were contemplating entry into administration from faculty ranks and had selected Administration 101 with the intent of exploring the career move.

The summer 2002 cohort was made up of twenty-eight men and thirty-six women. As in the case of the first cohort, participants were drawn from every type of community college (large and small, urban and rural, single- and multicollege districts) and represented every major ethnic group in the system. The cohort included multiple levels of administrative positions: twenty-eight individuals held titles of dean or above, with several assistant superintendents and vice presidents of student services and instruction represented. Seventeen participants had more than ten years' experience in community college administration.

Presenter Sample. There were fifteen program faculty, eight of whom served in both 2001 and 2002. These experts were drawn from the senior ranks of community college leaders and included a district chancellor; vice chancellors for budget, finance, and human resources; college presidents; and experienced chief instructional and student service officers. In addition, representatives from key California community college professional associations and agencies were invited to present selected topics. Presenters came from urban, rural, and suburban colleges, single- and multicampus districts, and were otherwise representative of community college administrators.

Data Analysis

Analysis of qualitative data for this project depended on a coding, categorizing, and theme-searching process. Written evaluation, interview, and focus group material underwent content analysis that required identifying themes and patterns that gave sense to the data. Frequency counts of recurring ideas or types of responses were used extensively to synthesize the data and identify key themes.

Analysis of the quantitative data derived from evaluation questionnaires for 2001 and 2002 used simple statistical summaries. Although the study did not focus primarily on comparing the experiences of the summer 2001 and 2002 cohorts, in some instances a comparison of ratings from both groups provided insights related to the program design and content. For instance, feedback from the first cohort on the structure of the session dealing with governance affected the presentation format for the second year, and the feedback from the second cohort validated the effectiveness of the change. By describing and analyzing the perspectives of both presenters and participants and integrating the data and results of the various methods, a formative evaluation of the Administration 101 program emerged.

Findings

Program curriculum was similar although not identical in 2001 and 2002. Topics added for the 2002 session included participative governance, accreditation, and legislative updates. The closing session for 2001 was focused on building community whereas that of 2002 focused on the theme of student retention.

Usefulness. Of the range of constructs modeled by the questionnaire, the measure dealing with usefulness was considered important because it constituted an overarching element in evaluating presentations and reflected participant perceptions about the long-term effects of each session. In 2001, 48 participants provided input on the usefulness measure; this represents a 74 percent response rate. For this session, the number of participants who rated this measure as "excellent" ranged from a low of 27 respondents (56 percent) for the topic on the role of the board of trustees to a high of 41 respondents (86 percent) for the closing session with the theme of building community. During the summer 2002 session, 49 respondents, a 77 percent response rate, offered ratings on final evaluations. For this session, the number of participants who rated the usefulness of presentations as excellent ranged from 20 (41 percent) for the topic on technology planning to a high of 46 (94 percent) for budget development.

Several factors account for the differences in ratings between the two sessions. Primarily, changes in presenters affected perceptions about the usefulness of the content. It is no accident that in 2002, the sessions that were rated most highly (budget development and participative governance) were also those given by two exceptionally articulate, witty, and effective communicators. In addition, the restructuring of the presentation on governance and the role of the board of trustees into a single integrated session in 2002 clearly enhanced perceptions about the session, with the number of respondents awarding excellent ratings rising from 28 (58 percent) and 27 (56 percent) in 2001 to 35 (71 percent) and 37 (76 percent) in 2002, respectively.

The amount of time allocated to the session also affected participants' perceptions of usefulness. For example, whereas most sessions were allotted half-day time blocks, several presentations were allotted one-hour time blocks. The short sessions typically received lower "excellent" ratings than longer sessions. For example, sessions on research and strategic planning (23 percent [$n = 11$]) in 2001, accreditation (52 percent [$n = 25$]), and technology planning (41 percent [n = 20]) in 2002 were each presented in a one-hour time block. Participant comments clarified that more time was needed on lower-rated topics to fully explore the complexities of the subject and to develop applications and case-study scenarios.

Final Program Evaluation. The final program evaluation form completed by all participants at the conclusion of the program provided a number of insights into the program's effects. To the query, "What do you like best about Administration 101?" participants' most positive responses centered on the array and variety of presentations and the opportunities to network. Other positive responses alluded to the quality of the presentations; the value of the instructional materials; the conference organization; and the conference arrangements, including accommodations and meals.

Content analysis of the written comments from both cohorts identified repeated requests for fewer but more in-depth sessions with more interaction (eighteen respondents in 2001 and seven in 2002). This result was echoed in follow-up focus discussion sessions in which all participants stated preferences for various types of interactive formats: small group work, discussions, question and answer, and role playing and simulations.

Participants reported that the use of PowerPoint presentations was also viewed as beneficial; the tool facilitated the organization of complex topics and note taking by participants. However, when PowerPoint was employed, it was viewed as critical to provide handouts that paralleled the presentations.

A comparison of the top-rated sessions by each cohort yields a few additional insights. Although the two program sessions between 2001 and 2002 were largely similar, each closing session presentation was unique. Interestingly, both of these—"Building Community" in 2001 and "Effective Student Retention Models" in 2002—were rated highly. This finding suggests the value of including "big picture" integrative topics that provide a balance to the curriculum emphasis on specific managerial aspects of community college administration.

On another note, in response to participant input from 2001, a session on successful participative governance models was added in 2002, and this received the second highest rating in 2002. Clearly, this session "hit a nerve" and will be retained. This outcome points to the value of using evaluation feedback to continually revise and update curriculum. Finally, two of the same presentations were rated in the top five by both cohorts: institutional dynamics and budget development. It is difficult to attribute these ratings solely to the content or usefulness measures because there was no clear pattern that emerged on the basis of these. Again, the factor that seems most obvious is the quality of the presentation itself. There is no substitute for excellent program faculty!

Findings based on participant evaluations and on focus group discussions clearly point to several program strengths. First, participants valued concrete, "real-leadership" case studies over lecture format presentations.

As one respondent commented on a written evaluation form, "Talking heads are deadly." In particular, participants expressed great appreciation for case studies based on presenters' professional and personal experiences. Data in this study clearly indicated that interactive methods are not only effective but also essential for an adult learning population made up of community college professionals. Repeatedly, in instances where presenters had successfully integrated interactive methods, participants were enthusiastic. A sampling of comments makes the point:

> Terrific! This was an effective blend of lessons learned from experts; interactive opportunity to explore our problem-solving skills and follow-up/review of group work to see the big picture, glean and take home ideas, and identify areas that need further work. The speaker's opening comment offered a great balanced perspective [2001 participant comment regarding the Instruction and Student Services presentation].

> Greatly enjoyed the interactivity; immense learning from colleagues [2002 participant comment for the Instruction and Student Services topic].

Second, participants responded well to program faculty drawn from the ranks of recognized leaders and experts in California community college governance and administration. Participants also indicated that networking activities available as an integral part of the program experience were a highlight of the entire program. Third, participants identified the intensive study format in a university setting and the useful resource materials provided (especially the Administration 101 resource notebook) as valuable to their learning process during the program and when they returned to the workplace. Finally, participants were impressed with the concise and well-organized presentations of technical information on complex administrative activities such as attendance-accounting requirements and the state program approval process.

Conclusions

The one unanimous recommendation that emerged from all focus groups was to design and conduct a follow-up "Administration 202" program. This result leads to the conclusion that the program met the expressed needs of the California community college administrative field for customized professional development. However, it also suggests that additional in-depth experiences should be added. Like any 101 course, initial exposure was provided in a number of topical areas. A more focused, intensive learning experience will build on the foundation provided by Administration 101.

One major proviso exists for the effective use of case studies: sufficient context, materials, and background must be provided to facilitate participant understanding. To be effective, case studies require a great deal of up-front development and structured monitoring. The value of using case studies should definitely be taken into account for any subsequent program development.

Reading materials and handouts were much valued, particularly when these were included in the resource binder that was sent to the participants weeks before the start of the program. Novice administrators especially appreciated the opportunity to acquaint themselves with the materials ahead of time. Based on survey results, participants appeared to extensively use the program materials for reference purposes in their work.

This study adds to the literature of community college leadership development approaches. McCauley (1986) pointed to the value of providing intermittent and limited training programs as one major pathway for facilitating the acquisition of administrative skills and competencies. Administration 101 represents a model for such a training concept, and this study points to the program elements that make it effective. One example is the program's manageable short-term intensive format. Similarly, the program's emphasis on peer networking shows the effects of learning from colleagues. Administration 101 thus offers a viable program model that substantiates selected professional development approaches discussed in the research literature (Bragg, 2000; Elsner, 1984; Laden, 1995).

References

Association of California Community College Administrators. *Administration 101: Curriculum Outline*. Sacramento: Association of California Community College Administrators, 2002.

Barnes, C., and others. "Community College Leadership Programs." Sacramento: Joint Committee of the California State University and the California Community Colleges on Leadership Programs, 1987. (ED 293 568)

Bragg, D. D. "Preparing Community College Deans to Lead Change." In D. Robillard, Jr. (ed.), *Dimensions of Managing Academic Affairs in the Community College*. New Directions for Community Colleges, no. 109. San Francisco: Jossey-Bass, 2000.

Chancellor's Task Force on California Community College Leadership. Report. Sacramento: California Community Colleges Chancellor's Office, Feb. 2002.

Elsner, P. "Meeting the Challenges with New Leadership Programs." In R. L. Alfred, P. A. Elsner, R. J. LeCroy, and N. Armes (eds.), *Emerging Roles for Community College Leaders*. New Directions for Community Colleges, no. 46. San Francisco: Jossey-Bass, 1984.

Laden, B. "The Role of Professional Associations in Developing Academic and Administrative Leaders." In J. Palmer and S. Katsinas (eds.), *Graduate and Continuing Education for Community College Leaders: What It Means Today*. New Directions for Community Colleges no. 95. San Francisco: Jossey-Bass, 1995.

McCauley, C. D. "Developmental Experiences in Managerial Work: A Literature Review." Technical Report no. 26. Greensboro, N.C.: Center for Creative Leadership, 1986.

Patton, M. Q. *Utilization-Focused Evaluation*. (3rd ed.) Thousand Oaks, Calif.: Sage Publications, 1997.

Rubin, H. J., and Rubin, I. S. *Qualitative Interviewing: The Art of Hearing Data.* Thousand Oaks, Calif.: Sage Publications, 1995.

Townsend, B. K., and Bassoppo-Moyo, S. "The Effective Community College Academic Administrator: Necessary Competencies and Attitudes." *Community College Review,* 1997, 25(2), 41–56.

CRISTINA CHIRIBOGA is vice president of instruction at Cuyamaca College, El Cajon, California.

To meet the unprecedented demand for well-prepared
leaders, a regional approach can be helpful that draws on
a range of providers, offering a variety of development
opportunities for aspiring and practicing leaders.

Leadership Development:
A Collaborative Approach

Constance M. Carroll, Martha Gandert Romero

In the latter half of the 1990s, the Accrediting Commission for Community
and Junior Colleges of the Western Association of Schools and Colleges
noted two alarming trends among two-year institutions in California,
Hawaii, American Samoa, Guam, the Commonwealth of the Northern
Marianas, the Republic of the Marshall Islands, the Federated States of
Micronesia, and the Republic of Palau. It is increasingly difficult to attract
and retain leaders, and turmoil within institutional governance has intensified: "The Commission, based upon its reading of visiting team reports to
scores of two year colleges in recent years, had witnessed stresses and
strains that reduced the ability of responsible college leaders to set sound
directions for their campuses" (2000, p. 6). The prevalence of these two
problems caused the commission to give them special attention.

In 1998, at the request of the commission's executive director, a group
of concerned commissioners, augmented by other community college leaders, soon structured themselves as a board of directors and incorporated
their effort as the Community College Leadership Development Initiatives
(CCLDI). Their goal was to discover the causes of these problems and to
devise strategies to solve them by strengthening leadership throughout the
western region. In this chapter, we describe the development and implementation of the CCLDI, which may serve as a model of collaborative leadership development for community colleges elsewhere.

Problem Definition

The first order of business for the CCLDI board was to ascertain the full nature and extent of these problems. The board commissioned a regionwide survey of community college CEOs and faculty leaders to determine their views and also obtained information from the Community College League of California, the University of Hawaii, the California Community Colleges Chancellor's Office, the American Association of Community Colleges, and other organizations. The findings supported and intensified the CCLDI board's concerns (Community College Leadership Development Initiatives, 2000). Some highlights follow.

In 1977, 28 percent of CEOs of community colleges in California had held their position for ten years or more. By 1997, however, that proportion had been reduced to 13 percent. Moreover, the average tenure for a California community college CEO in 1997 was 4.4 years compared with 7.5 years nationally. Reports of CEOs surviving as little as two or three years and departing as the result of severe governance and political controversy were more troubling. Similar patterns were found in community colleges in Hawaii and the Western Pacific (Community College Leadership Development Initiatives, 2000).

Faculty survey responses indicated that faculty members found it increasingly burdensome to assume leadership positions, both because of the lack of training for the positions and because of inadequate support. Of greatest concern to CCLDI was that few of the faculty respondents expressed an interest in pursuing administrative positions. This reluctance in the context of existing leadership problems and smaller and smaller pools of qualified candidates for leadership positions at all levels intensified CCLDI's concern, especially in view of the massive number of administrative and faculty retirements on the horizon, both in the western region and nationally.

In its first monograph, the CCLDI described itself as sounding an alarm: "Our alarm spoke to the mounting difficulties faced by community college leadership, at all levels, within the western region. We were worried that, without stronger leadership, our ability to educate the 1,500,000 students who depend upon the public two-year colleges would be endangered" (Community College Leadership Development Initiatives, 2000, p. 6).

The group speculated that

> the community college "movement" has faltered. In earlier decades the word "movement" bespoke a belief in the responsiveness to community needs as well as professional and disciplinary dictates; exaltation of teaching and advising as the critical characteristics of excellence in community college faculty; a willingness and capacity to teach students who come from many different educational backgrounds and levels of preparation. These values remain alive on community college campuses but they are now too often crowded out by

a growing emphasis on identification with special interest groups and a growth in adversarial relationships among groups. . . . there is no longer an emotional commitment to institutional mission on many campuses strong enough to temper many parochial demands [Community College Leadership Development Initiatives, 2000, p. 7].

The CCLDI Plan

CCLDI planned to address these problems by providing opportunities for leadership training and to ensure that those entering the leadership "pipeline" and those already in leadership positions were fully prepared for the challenges and opportunities of the modern community college. Myriad uses of technology, growing diversity of the student population, economic development needs of local communities, the effects of global interdependence, ethical considerations, alternative financial strategies, and many other issues must be addressed by today's community college presidents, governing board members, administrators, and faculty members. To address such a broad range of issues in a manner that would provide leadership training for an extremely diverse population, CCLDI envisioned that a community college leadership institute must develop the following five program components:

A *doctoral fellows program:* an interdisciplinary and cocurricular approach to provide for focus and discussion among doctoral students enrolled in participating universities who are committed to community college leadership
A *leadership fellows program:* a multiyear program for promising leaders already at work in community colleges who aspire to increased levels of leadership and either already have or do not seek a doctoral degree. These individuals would be selected and nominated by their colleges.
A *certificate program for new community college leaders:* a program designed for community college faculty, midlevel managers, or trustees who have had no formal preparation in community college issues and are not interested in degree programs but who would benefit from a coherent set of courses addressing such issues as community college history, pedagogy, governance, finance, and conflict resolution.
An *intensive summer workshop in community college leadership:* a program for existing community college practitioners at all levels designed to provide a two- to three-week experience in exploring community college leadership issues or in a shorter more focused format for selected groups—for example, CEOs, faculty leaders, or other groups
Information dissemination and research: a vehicle for providing up-to-date research and information about community colleges, including the dissemination of the results of current doctoral studies and leadership development opportunities

This ambitious program would be characterized by two important dynamics. First, scholars from the sponsoring organizations and practitioners from the community colleges would interact in all components of the program to ensure that the programs are both academically rigorous and grounded in real community college experience. Second, the interaction between scholars and practitioners would produce new ongoing networks for collegial exchange, thereby enlivening and expanding dialogue and discussion of community college issues.

These ends were not likely to be achieved by one giant centralized supplier located on a single campus and serving a complex of program elements over a huge geographical area. Rather, the CCLDI favored a coordinated but decentralized arrangement that took advantage of already existing institutions and individuals who might want to collaborate and be of service.

Key Partnership

CCLDI wanted a respected institution capable of addressing all aspects of leadership development that would take responsibility for shaping the program, convening other institutions of higher education to participate, coordinating the effort, and providing an avenue for advice and participation by practitioners. Interestingly, after many meetings and interactions, it became clear that no public university wished to undertake the responsibility for a program of this magnitude. When the CCLDI issued a formal request for proposals to head this venture, only private institutions responded. One of these institutions, Claremont Graduate University (CGU), responded with enthusiasm, vision, and strong commitment, with the result that the CCLDI and CGU entered into a partnership. In April 2000, CCLDI and CGU signed a memorandum of understanding, and the idea finally became reality. Subsequently, the University of California-Irvine, San Diego State University, and California State University at Sacramento joined CGU as participating regional partners. The University of California-Los Angeles (UCLA) became a key partner as the host of the doctoral fellows program, and the research collaboration included St. Mary's College, the University of Southern California, The Fielding Institute, CGU, UCLA, San Diego State University, the University of San Diego, and the University of Hawaii. Also working with CCLDI in supporting research on community colleges are California State University-Stanislaus and the University of California-Riverside.

Verifying and Refining the Concept

In June 2000, CCLDI convened a special design workshop at CGU that created a unique opportunity for scholars and practitioners from the western region to discuss in detail the problems, issues, and practical considerations involved in providing leadership training for both new and incumbent community college leaders. Community college trustees, presidents, and faculty members, university professors and administrators, researchers, and others met for several days of intensive discussion and planning. This meeting reaffirmed the planning directions of CCLDI. The elements to be included in a leadership program would require participants to look inward toward a leader's values and leadership style and outward toward the institutional environment. Twelve fundamental elements of leadership were identified, and these formed the basis for the implementation of the leadership programs. These elements of leadership are as follows:

> Developing self-awareness and accepting criticism as an element of growth
> Cultivating communication skills
> Working with individuals and groups through collaboration, facilitation, and conflict resolution
> Cultivating leadership in students, staff, faculty, administrators, and trustees
> Understanding, integrating, and shaping institutional culture
> Managing internal institutional functions such as finance, personnel, legal affairs, and facilities operations
> Mastering planning, organizational development, and decision making aimed at improving quality
> Nurturing ethical behavior and ethical analysis
> Dedicating oneself and one's institution to teaching and learning
> Embracing and valuing diversity
> Attending to the external environment, including its educational, political, and economic dimensions; media relations; and civic responsibility
> Valuing the history and mission of community colleges and higher education, and understanding state structures
> [Community College Leadership Development Initiative, 2001, pp. 5–7].

This set of twelve characteristics is dynamic. The set emerged from the workshop conducted in March 2001, but subsequent sessions and subsequent circumstances will no doubt cause the list to grow or change to meet the changing context. For example, in the first Leadership Seminar (to be discussed in the next section), the concept of "good work" provided an additional value.

Program Implementation

Two key factors have helped this initiative progress quickly. First, community colleges have a strong tradition of working together to solve problems. In California, within the 108-college system, many examples exist of collaboratives where groups of colleges come together to develop joint programs, to contract with outside vendors, or to share training opportunities. Similarly, the colleges in Hawaii have undertaken cooperative ventures for many years. More recently, in the Western Pacific, through the Pacific Postsecondary Education Council, coordination and cooperation between the six-member institutions have been growing. Thus, it was relatively easy for colleges from throughout the region to join together in supporting the work of the CCLDI and its foundation (Community College Leadership Development Initiatives Foundation). Second, from the start, CGU has taken a position as the lead institution. Its role is to serve as the catalyst for the development of new programs. The goal has never been for the CCLDI or CGU to be the sole provider of programs or services. The problem as defined is large and diverse and can best be met through many programs with different foci, time frames, and target leadership groups. CCLDI's Web site (http://www.cgu.edu/ccldi) carries information about current programs and adds links to the programs in other institutions as those are implemented.

In fall 2000, CCLDI appointed a former community college president with extensive experience as both a practitioner and scholar as director charged with responsibility for implementing the new leadership program. Within the first full year of operation, two programs have made strong beginnings, and two others are being actively developed. In all these programs, the twelve attributes and the five program priorities have been development guideposts.

Leadership Academy. In July 2002, twelve campuses brought teams of leaders that included trustees, CEOs, senior administrators, and classified managers (forty-seven in all) to the first Leadership Academy at CGU. These forty-seven leadership fellows entered into a weeklong residential program of intensive leadership and organizational skill building. The week began with a series of individual leadership assessment activities and progressed to organizational and systems development issues; problem-solving sessions that included a variety of skill-building opportunities were employed. The academy faculty included nationally recognized leaders from community colleges across the country and leadership scholars from CGU. Among the major themes explored were "good work" and "connective leadership." All sessions allowed participants to explore their commitment to the work of community colleges. Evenings were structured to allow participants to debrief the day's content with others who shared similar campus roles.

The good-work emphasis allowed participants to explore how moral and ethical standards coupled with high-level performance and social responsibility give meaning to the work we accomplish as individuals in our various roles. The individual leader doing good work in the context of the college emerged as the unifying thread for the entire week. The session on connective leadership allowed the participants to examine their own leadership styles in light of the psychological factors that make for effective leadership. Sessions were conducted on change as seen through multiple lenses, diversity as a dynamic that colors all perceptions of our society regardless of color or ethnic background, and planning and decision systems coupled with decision-making styles within the collegiate setting. The final session explored leadership traditions in the Pacific Islands and the lessons they might provide in contemporary settings.

The goal of the Leadership Academy is to provide a common set of experiences that professionals across all levels of the participating institutions can use to enhance leadership at their institutions. The curriculum responds to the twelve leadership elements identified by practitioners and noted above. The program piloted in the first Leadership Academy was evaluated positively by observers and participants and has become the cornerstone for continuing leadership development activities.

In addition to the program for leadership skill development, the noncredit leadership program provides opportunities for fellows to continue to meet in policy seminars once a month with CCLDI's regional partners, the University of California-Irvine, San Diego State University, and California State University-Sacramento. Seminars address topics such as finance, the difference between assessment and accountability, issues imbedded in the teaching-learning paradigm shift, dilemmas of internal and external community building, and human resource law and diversity. This ongoing network of fellows engaging everyday issues reinforces the community of leaders established in the academy and extends itself continuously to the participating community colleges as it reaches back to the academy experience.

A capstone event for the leadership fellows year is designed to help participants synthesize their experience. Using a format that the fellows create themselves, the intent is to help them see the relationship between policy, theory, and research and leadership practice.

Doctoral Fellows Program. The first doctoral fellows program commenced in fall 2002 at UCLA. The fellows program brings together advanced doctoral-level students interested in the community college to share research and engage in more concentrated discussions on community college leadership. Sixteen doctoral fellows from eight universities in the region have been selected as CCLDI doctoral fellows. Thirteen of the sixteen fellows are already employed at community colleges. The fellows met three times during the 2002–03 academic year and will discuss research topics of interest to community colleges and share research interests as they prepare their doctoral-level work. The network developed among the doctoral fellows and their sponsoring institutions will, we hope, bring the interests of the community colleges and of research institutions into closer alignment so that both scholars and practitioners benefit from regular and focused interaction. Leaders developed through these ongoing connections will, we are confident, form a long-term support network as they assume positions of greater responsibility.

Community College Certificate and Advanced Programs. With encouragement from CCLDI, numerous institutions in California and Hawaii are developing new programs or expanding current programs to create certificate and master's and doctoral degree programs in community college teaching and leadership. California State University-Stanislaus now offers a certificate program in community college administration, and California State University-Sacramento has for several years provided a certificate in community college teaching. University of Hawaii and San Diego State University professors are beginning to exchange teaching opportunities. A collaborative of institutions that have expressed an interest in working together to offer doctoral programs to the institutions in the Western Pacific are discussing how they might deliver programs to these isolated islands. Joint doctoral programs are now under development between campuses of the University of California and the California State University. One such example involves University of California-Davis and California State University's Sacramento and Sonoma campuses.

Research and Information Dissemination. One of the goals of CCLDI is to bring researchers and practitioners into closer alignment so that research conducted on community colleges more closely meets the needs of practitioners as they make decisions. Twelve universities have indicated an interest in developing a common research agenda that will better serve community college practitioners. As of this writing, several doctoral students have begun to put together an inventory of the research currently under way either at research institutions or at associations and other research organizations that focus on the community colleges. Another doctoral project is preparing to survey the field of community college practitioners about their use of research findings, the accessibility of such research results, and requests for research that go unmet. CCLDI submitted the results of these efforts for publication in 2003.

CCLDI has put in place mechanisms to disseminate research results in more accessible forms and within a shorter time frame than are possible through journals and books. CCLDI convenes a group of research university representatives in the West to share timely information and discuss possible research topics. In a recent study conducted by our research staff, we discovered that practitioners prefer to get their information electronically or by newsletters that synthesize information and provide a source for further follow-up if needed. Thus, we have begun a quarterly newsletter (we are considering monthly newsletters as funding becomes available) that synthesizes recent research findings. Of course, the staff at CCLDI also participate in conferences and forums. The Leadership Academy, policy seminars, and occasional workshops use the most current research available.

CCLDI also has plans to develop a knowledge management system that will allow practitioners to interact with other practitioners on issues and writings of common interest.

Conclusion

CCLDI is an attempt to bring new meaning to the notion of comprehensive leadership development by responding to the needs of faculty, trustees, classified staff, and administrators by focusing on both skill development and mastery of the substantive issues of the day. CCLDI has developed programming for both aspiring leaders and leaders already in place using a variety of development formats, from one-day workshops to weeklong academies to monthly seminars to ongoing coaching relationships to certificate, master's, and doctoral programs. Striving to make a better connection between the research desired by practitioners and the research undertaken in graduate schools, CCLDI has worked with a full range of leadership development capacity already in existence (mostly graduate schools of education at public and private universities). Finally, CCLDI has provided services over a large geographical space, continuously interacting with both community colleges and the sources (including potential sources) of leadership development services so that program offerings evolve with changing circumstances.

Through its initial operations, CCLDI has been able to demonstrate that each of these goals is realizable. Sufficient success has been achieved that we conclude that this model can work wherever a set of community colleges and a collection of leadership development providers wish to pursue it. As noted throughout this volume, the need for community college leadership development is vast. One way in which this issue can be addressed on a reasonably large scale is with an approach like that of CCLDI. We hope others will join in similar adventures.

References

Community College Leadership Development Initiatives at Claremont Graduate University. "Meeting New Leadership Challenges in the Community Colleges." Claremont, Calif.: Community College Leadership Development Initiatives, 2000. [http://www.cgu.edu/ccldi/toc.htm]. Retrieved July 9, 2003.

Community College Leadership Development Initiatives at Claremont Graduate University. "Profiles for Progress: Preparing Community College Leaders for a New Era." Claremont, Calif.: Community College Leadership Development Initiatives, 2001. [http://www.cgu.edu/ccldi/toc.htm]. Retrieved July 9, 2003.

CONSTANCE M. CARROLL is president of San Diego Mesa College.

MARTHA GANDERT ROMERO is director of Community College Leadership Development Initiatives at Claremont Graduate University, Claremont, California.

9

The traditional means of preparing community college leaders are disjointed and in many cases ill suited to meet the challenges leaders will face through the beginning decades of the twenty-first century. Community colleges must take a proactive role in the development of their future leaders.

In-House Leadership Development: Placing the Colleges Squarely in the Middle

William E. Piland, David B. Wolf

The nation's community colleges recently celebrated their one hundredth anniversary. With the founding of Joliet Junior College in 1901 in Joliet, Illinois, an entirely new higher education institution emerged in our country. This unique type of institution requires unique leaders. Yet, leadership development over the decades has paralleled the development of secondary school leaders, usually without a credential requirement.

Secondary school principals and superintendents were the first junior college leaders. Their preparation, including on-the-job training and graduate education, may have served our colleges well as they expanded and met educational needs not served by universities in the first half of the twentieth century. When junior colleges became comprehensive community colleges during the 1960s and 1970s, they became complex institutions of higher education and more like their university peers than the public schools from which they sprang. However, community colleges could be served by taking some leadership development practices from the K–12 sector, such as those requiring formal training for new faculty that emphasizes understanding of institutional mission and history, student characteristics, and appropriate classroom practices.

Universities, on the other hand, could not provide role models for community college leadership development. University leaders were frequently selected because of their records as scholars. Scholarly productivity, including research, writing, grants, and theory building, were, and continue to be, the highly desirable qualities sought in university leaders. University leaders' training has been heavily weighted in favor of on-the-job training (movement through the academic ranks and through administrative and quasi-administrative positions within the university) plus short-term, targeted leadership development offered by prestigious universities or professional associations. Obviously, these leadership qualities do not match the missions and functions of community colleges.

As we enter a new century, we urge the pursuit of a new leadership development paradigm, one that places the individual community colleges in the middle of the action. The leaders we need—in terms of quality and quantity—will result only when the institutions themselves make leadership development a high priority, invest in appropriate programming, and work cooperatively with other suppliers.

Leadership Development in the Past

Historically, community college leadership development has included a mix of on-the-job training, graduate education, and short-term, unconnected leadership training opportunities. The on-the-job training was, and still often is, unorganized and entirely dependent on the aggressiveness of the individual administrator or faculty leader and the opportunities that presented themselves. Some leaders in middle-management positions and in faculty leadership roles have made it a point to learn more than just the rudimentary aspects of their roles. These educators were pegged as "comers" who someday would seek higher-level leadership positions. Others simply learned their jobs and after a period of time felt they were ready to move up (and this happens commonly). Chris McCarthy's chapter, "Learning on the Job: Moving from Faculty to Administration," traces the journey of one such leader through the ranks.

As these emerging leaders gained leadership-related experience in the community colleges, they typically enrolled in graduate programs, usually at the doctoral level, but sometimes at the master's level, to achieve an advanced degree that has become the coin of the realm. One of us can recall asking his dean of instruction when he was a division director if he should pursue a doctoral degree. The dean advised, "If you want a high-level administrative position, you should because boards of trustees like to announce that they hired 'Dr. So-and-So' for those big-money jobs." There was no mention made of the skills and competencies to be learned in a doctoral program. This response has been symptomatic of the disconnect between university-based leadership preparation programs and the needs within the field. Betty Duvall has related some of the difficulties with university leadership development efforts in her chapter on the "Role of Universities in Leadership Development."

Finally, some emerging community college leaders actively pursue professional development opportunities through professional associations. George Boggs in his chapter, "Leadership Context for the Twenty-First Century," has itemized the programs offered by the American Association of Community Colleges. State-level associations also provide leadership development opportunities. Cristina Chiriboga's chapter, "Administration 101: Evaluation of a Professional Development Program," depicts one such program. Many community college leaders have difficulty pursuing these opportunities because of the demanding nature of their positions, and at times, these programs do not mesh with the needs of individual leaders.

The biggest difficulty with all of these efforts is that they are disconnected. There is no relationship between what is occurring in the way of on-the-job training, university graduate programs, and leadership development through professional organizations. In addition, it is incumbent on an aspiring leader to try and make the pieces fit. This is a classic case of the individual taking on the system to make it work for him or her. Sometimes it works, and sometimes the system prevails and community college leaders end up with a hodge-podge of skills and competencies.

The inherent nature of leading in a community college is almost always absent from the "design" (if that term can be properly applied to the various independent efforts). For example, one such characterization is directly described in the March and Weiner chapter titled "Leadership Blues." The nature of leadership in community colleges needs continued deep, thoughtful, summative exploration to provide an evolving foundation for leadership training programs. Community college leadership has its own set of problems, challenges, and demands. The dynamic nature of community colleges, their place in the nation's higher education system, and their extremely diverse student bodies make community colleges unique institutions of learning. Duplicating existing programs that prepare educational leaders without thoroughly understanding these institutions will simply perpetuate an inadequate system to meet present and future leadership needs.

What of the community colleges in the development of their leaders, one may ask? We are sorry to report that they are "missing in action." Far too many of our colleges do not take an active role in developing leaders for their colleges. Some colleges have small sporadic programs to develop their own leaders through in-house internships or staff development activities. These programs tend to be poorly funded, loosely organized, and add-on responsibilities for someone in the organization. Colleges with such programs do not see themselves as preparing the next generation of community college leaders. Rather, each college is developing leaders for an individual college, not for the field. Investing in their own leaders may be acceptable as long as the investment in time and resources is minimal. Investing in leaders whose careers will likely take them to other colleges? No way!

Community College Role in Leadership Development

Community colleges must become proactive in the development of leaders. They need to take responsibility for playing a major role in producing the next generation of community college leaders. They need not take on this responsibility alone. Other institutions and organizations have roles to play (McPhail, 2000). However, community colleges must be the nexus of this effort.

Let us be clear about the consequences of a failure of community colleges to assume this central responsibility. Much has been said in this and other volumes about both the increasing complexity of community colleges and the risks associated with leading them. The steady decline in the willingness of talented faculty to assume leadership positions, the decline in the number of candidates presenting themselves for middle and senior administrative assignments, and the relatively poor preparation that many of these candidates have received are all indices of the current problem. Without meaningful intervention, this reduction in the size and quality of leadership pools will continue. We note that universities, and more recently school districts, have turned to former politicians, business leaders, and government officials to fill senior positions. Although persons with wholly different experience may bring something important to leadership positions under special circumstances, we would not like to see community college trustees turning to these alternatives because persons with superb community college preparation were simply not available. This bodes poorly for achieving the mission of the colleges and for the success of millions of students.

But exciting responses to this challenge are in evidence. Listed below are ideas that can be, and in some cases are being, pursued by community colleges. They include a wide range of actions in size and scope. They are all community college centered and within the purview of an individual college, and sometimes groups of colleges, to undertake.

Formalize a leadership development policy and program to prepare future leaders among faculty, support staff, and administrators. Secure board approval of the policy and support for the program with appropriate resources. Assign the program to a responsible individual, perhaps the staff development officer. Elements of policy that would be worthy of attention include the use of sabbaticals for leadership training, the right of administrators to some sort of extended leave for such activities, and financial support for persons pursuing longer-term leadership programs (summer workshops, advanced degrees).

Establish a leadership development committee made up of administrators, faculty, and support staff to guide the program. It is highly desirable that the chancellor or president serve on this committee.

Institute a formal mentoring program for emerging leaders in the community college. Mentors should work closely with their "mentees" to diagnose needs, prescribe experiences and activities to meet those needs, assess the progress and development of mentees, and teach the future leaders the subtleties of leading a community college (Jensen, Giles, and Kirklin, 2000). Mentors and mentees should receive some types of recognition and reward for their efforts.

Leaders in community colleges must proactively identify and cultivate future leaders among the faculty, administrators, and support staff in their college. It is imperative that people of color and women are targeted for inclusion in all leadership training programs. The ranks of community college leaders must be made more diverse for our colleges to serve an increasingly diverse student body preparing for their places within a diverse society (Ebbers, Gallisath, Rockel, and Coyan, 2000). Both through appropriate policy and programming consistent with policy, the promotion of a diverse leadership corps must be pursued.

Carefully constructed programs that are implemented at the institutional level (individual campus or perhaps the local district or system) may be the best way to meet particular demands. For example, Vaughan and Weisman (Chapter Five) have presented ideas about the development of presidential leaders at the local community college level. Cooper and Pagotto (Chapter Three) demonstrate how a locally operated program (employing expertise from the nearby university) focused on the development of leadership skills within the faculty can be fashioned. We strongly urge that local programs develop useful case studies from the experience of the particular institutions. These should be "unvarnished" stories that carry the richness of important leadership circumstances. The case studies should form the core of the curriculum and could be made available to other colleges and universities for educational purposes.

Colleges in contiguous geographical regions can form a Leadership Development Consortium to share the experiences and resources required for a more comprehensive leadership development effort. Giving potential leaders experiences in more than one college is highly valuable for their development. Sharing experiences, costs, and resources can strengthen each college's leadership development program. In addition, a core of leaders will be developed within a wider geographical region, producing a pool of potential leaders for leadership openings that occur within that region.

Community colleges must take the lead role in fostering the development of new leadership training opportunities or improving existing ones that involve universities and professional associations or organizations. The disconnect between university leadership programs and the needs of leaders in the field must be addressed (Vaughan, 2001). Current community college leaders should take an active role in advisory committees for university programs. If no advisory committee exists, community college leaders must begin to raise questions as to why not. Community colleges can bring pressures to bear on universities, both public and private, to address their leadership needs. Of course, community colleges cannot dictate, nor should they, to their university partners. They can take an active role in shaping programs and services that meet their needs, however. When the community colleges sponsor their own leadership training programs, they bring an important asset to discussions with universities. The colleges can seek linkages with graduate institutions that attempt to mesh programs together to avoid duplication and fill in gaps. Both types of institutions can then build on their strengths and work together to offer a valuable leadership development resource.

The same notion holds true for professional organizations, especially those formed at the state level. Community college leaders can bring together the leaders of these organizations, with the university program leaders, to build a comprehensive leadership development program. In this scenario, there are now three major partners working together to form a gestalt that is far more powerful than any one of the partners. Professional organizations and universities often work together to offer educational programs and experiences for professionals in the field. Sometimes graduate credit, continuing education units, and degree credit are offered for these experiences. With the addition of representatives from the local community colleges, the capacity will exist to ensure that these experiences are meshed with the leadership preparation offered by the individual community colleges. The Community College Leadership Development Initiatives described by Carroll and Romero in Chapter Eight provides one model to form a powerful and effective consortium of university, state, and community college interests across an area involving more than one state.

Conclusion

Obtaining talented, properly prepared leaders is one of the major problems—some would say *the* major problem—facing community colleges at the beginning of the new century. Providing support for leaders in situ and bringing new people—especially talented folks who without a convincing argument and opportunities for preparation would never give leadership a second thought—to the challenges of leading are both of great urgency.

Achieving these ends in sufficient measure will not result from exclusive dependence on the traditional source of leadership training, graduate schools of education. Furthermore, the complexity and dynamism of the realm of community college leaders does not mesh well with the preferences of graduate faculty. Professional organizations, too, have severe limits on the programming they can provide.

Leading is extremely important. It is hard work. Leaders do not just happen. Excellent leadership results from the combination of motivated talent, the right leadership opportunity, and appropriate preparation. Are the community colleges themselves ready to do something about the one element they can reasonably control?

References

Ebbers, L. H., Gallisath, G., Rockel, V., and Coyan, M. N. "The Leadership Institute for a New Century: LINCing Women and Minorities into Tomorrow's Community College Leadership Roles." *Community College Journal of Research and Practice,* 2000, 24(5), 375–382.

Jensen, R., Giles, R., and Kirklin, P. *Insider's Guide to Community College Administration.* Annapolis Junction: Md.: Community College Press, 2000.

McPhail, C. J. "Transforming Community College Leadership Preparation: A Cohort Leadership Learning Model." Unpublished paper, Morgan State University, 2000. (ED 449 852)

Vaughan, G. B. "Developing Community College Leaders for the Future: Crisis or Opportunity." Unpublished paper, North Carolina State University at Raleigh, 2001. (ED 457 873)

WILLIAM E. PILAND *is professor of postsecondary education, San Diego State University; before becoming a university professor, he was a community college administrator for ten years.*

DAVID B. WOLF *is executive director emeritus, Accrediting Commission for Community and Junior Colleges, Western Association of Schools and Colleges.*

10

This chapter describes a sample of nondegree and degree programs currently offered to administrators, staff, and faculty in community college leadership.

Leadership Development Programs

Karen A. Kim

Programs for this listing were selected from many described in recent documents of the Educational Resource Information Center database. Neither this abbreviated program listing nor the information contained in each program description is intended to be comprehensive. Please contact leadership programs directly to obtain full information.

National Programs

The following programs, sponsored by national organizations and associations, offer a variety of leadership development opportunities for community college administrators and faculty.

Chair Academy
        Academy for Leadership and Development
        Gary Filan
        Executive Director
        145 N. Centennial Way
        Mesa, AZ 85201
        E-mail: chair.academy@mcmail.maricopa.edu
        Web site: http://www.mc.maricopa.edu/other/chair
        Target Audience. Community college administrators and faculty
        Program Description. A skills-based program begins with a five-day residential training, followed by a yearlong mentored practicum experience, and concluded by a five-day residential training. Nine hours of credit is available to participants seeking a master's or doctoral degree.

Founding and Participants. Founded in 1992, this program offers ten to twelve sessions annually with fifty-five to sixty participants enrolled in each session. The program has three thousand graduates worldwide.

Costs. $1,485. Customized statewide or collegewide programs are also available at lower program fees.

American Council on Education Fellows Program
  One Dupont Circle, N.W.
  Washington, DC 20036–1193
  Phone: (202) 939–9420; fax: (202) 785–8056
  E-mail: fellows@ace.nche.edu
  Web site: http://www.acenet.edu/programs/fellows
  Target Audience. Experienced faculty and administrators aspiring to senior positions
  Program Description. Participants spend one year on the campus of a host institution working under the mentorship of a team of experienced administrators to pursue various projects that coincide with their own interests and those of their home and host institutions. Participation also includes three weeklong national seminars, visits to other campuses, attendance at national meetings, and contact with a national network of higher education leaders.
  Founding and Participants. Founded in 1965, this program has fourteen hundred graduates. About thirty-five new fellows are selected annually.

Association of Community College Trustees
  Narcisa A. Polonio, Director
  Board Leadership Services
  1233 20th St., N.W., Suite 605
  Washington, D.C. 20036
  Phone: (202) 775–4667; fax: (202) 223–1297
  E-mail: npolonio@acct.org
  Web site: http://www.acct.org
  Target Audience. Members of community college governing boards
  Program Description. The Association of Community College Trustees board retreats last one and a half days, and retreat topics such as budget and finance, governance, community partnerships, and the effects of technology are facilitated by national community college experts at any suitable on- or off-campus location.

Executive Leadership Institute
  Brenda Beckman
  League for Innovation in the Community College
  4505 East Chandler Blvd., Suite 250
  Phoenix, AZ 85048

Phone: (520) 299–0939; fax: (520) 299–8822

E-mail: bmbeckman@aol.com

Web site: http://www.league.org/eli

Target Audience. Senior administrators in a leadership position within a community college who are qualified for a presidency by their educational and experiential background

Program Description. This is a weeklong program that helps potential community college presidents, or those in transition, to review their abilities and interests, to refine their skills, and to participate in discussions on leadership with outstanding community college leaders from North America.

Founding and Participants. Founded in 1988, this program has more than 450 graduates. Each program offering enrolls no more than thirty-eight participants.

Costs: $1,800

Future Leaders Institute

American Association of Community Colleges

One Dupont Circle, N.W., Suite 410

Washington, DC 20036

Phone: (202) 728–0200; fax: (202) 833–2467

E-mail: fli@aacc.nche.edu

Web site: http://www.aacc.nche.edu

Target Audience. Vice presidents, deans, directors, and those with similar responsibilities

Program. A five-day leadership seminar gives future leaders exposure and training in the skills, activities, knowledge, and attitudes necessary for successful twenty-first century community college leadership. It includes sessions in team building, conflict resolution, legal issues, personnel motivation, ethics, and other relevant issues.

Founding. Founded in 2003

Costs. Estimated at $1,610

National Institute for Leadership Development Leaders Institutes

Carrole A. Wolin, President

1202 W. Thomas Road

Phoenix College

Phoenix, AZ 85013

Phone: (602) 285–7727

E-mail: nild@nildleaders.org

Web site: http://www.nildleaders.org

Target Audience. Women administrators and faculty in higher education

Program Description. This five-day intensive institute emphasizes whole-person leadership perspectives, followed by one year of mentoring on an institutional project pertinent to participants' institutions. Customized presentations, workshops, and training are conducted regularly, and yearly reunions are offered at the American Association of Community Colleges annual convention and at the National Institute for Leadership Development (NILD)-American Association of Women in Community Colleges national conference.

Founding and Participants. Founded in 1981, NILD has more than forty-four hundred graduates. Three to four sessions with fifty participants each are offered between January and May each year.

Costs. $1,175 ($25 nonrefundable application fee included)

Regional Programs

The following workshops and seminars are offered by regional associations and universities, bringing together community college leaders from different campuses to gain professional development and to develop leadership skills.

Annual League Convention
   Community College League of California
   2017 O Street
   Sacramento, CA 95814
   Phone: (916) 444–8641; fax: (916) 444–2954
   E-mail: cclc@ccleague.org
   Web site: http://www.ccleague.org/ted.htm
   Target Audience. Trustees, administrators, staff, faculty, and students
   Program Description. Orientation workshops for trustees and student trustees; an annual legislative conference teaching trustees, administrators, faculty, staff, and students about major legislative issues and how to advocate for community colleges with the legislature; and a workshop for classified staff leadership cosponsored by the California Community College Classified Senate.

Community Colleges Leadership Development Initiatives
   Martha Romero
   Claremont Graduate University
   250 W. First Ave.
   Claremont, CA 91711
   Phone: (909) 447–1289
   E-mail: Martha.romero@cgu.edu
   Web site: http://www.cgu.edu/cldi
   Target Audience. Community college professionals

Program Description. The Community College Leadership Development Initiatives offers programs to develop community college leadership, to disseminate research, and to help doctoral students to learn more about community college leadership.

Founding. Founded in 2001

Costs. Currently no cost to participants

North Carolina Community College Leadership Program
    Kim Wyatt
    P.O. Box 1287
    Lexington, NC 27293–1287
    Web site: http://www.netpath.net/~lrc/NCCCLP.htm
    Target Audience. Employees of the North Carolina community college system
    Program Description. The North Carolina Community College Leadership Program (NCCCLP) is a seven-month program that provides leadership training through professional development of those interested in issues such as budget control and collaborative approaches to problem solving.
    Founding. Founded in 1989, NCCCLP originated under the auspices of the North Carolina Chapter of the American Association of Women in Community Colleges.

Community College Program

The following program is offered by a community college district to provide leadership development for administrators and faculty.

Consortium Leadership and Renewal Academy
    Jesse Jones
    North Texas Community College Consortium
    P.O. Box 311337
    University of North Texas
    Denton, TX 76203–1337
    Phone: (940) 565–4035
    E-mail: jjones@unt.edu or syoung@unt.edu
    Web site: http://www.unt.edu/ntccc
    Target Audience. Entry-level and midlevel administrators and faculty of the North Texas Community College Consortium
    Program Description. The Consortium Leadership and Renewal Academy is a yearlong regional leadership information, development, and renewal program that offers basic skills for those who have had minimal administrative experience and renewal opportunities for veteran administrators.
    Cost. $1,500

Continuing Education Programs Offered by Universities

The following university-sponsored programs provide a variety of workshops and online courses that do not require students to be enrolled in graduate degree programs within the institution, although some listings do offer the opportunity to count credits toward a master's degree within their program.

Community College Leadership Initiative Consortium
    Higher Education, Educational Leadership, and Policy Studies
    Iowa State University
    N232B Lagomarcino Hall
    Ames, IA 50011–3195
    Phone: (515) 294–9628; fax: (515) 294–4942
    Web site: http://www.educ.iastate.edu/elps/hged/clicdes.htm
    Target Audience. Upper-level and middle-management administrators
    Program Description. Training is provided in areas of management and supervision, current issues in the community college system, and networking opportunities to enhance communication between educational institutions. The program meets Iowa certification for administrator evaluator approval. Participants have the option of receiving additional graduate credit on completing the course.
    Founding. Founded in 1995

Community College Professional Education
    Antioch University McGregor
    Community College Management Department
    800 Livermore St.
    Yellow Springs, OH 45387–1609
    Phone: (937) 769–1890; fax: (937) 769–1806
    E-mail: Iris Weisman, iweisman@mcgregor.edu
    Web site: http://www.mcgregor.edu/CCM/cpe/index.html
    Progam Description. Customized continuing professional education programs combine on-site and online training or totally online experiences. Program participants may convert up to ten credits of professional development courses toward the M.A. in management, community college management track.

Community College Teaching and Learning Online
    University of Illinois, Urbana-Champaign
    Department of Human Resource Education
    345 College of Education, MC-708

1310 S. Sixth St.
Champaign, IL 61820
Phone: (217) 333–0807
E-mail: hre@uiuc.edu
Web site: http://www.hre.uiuc.edu/online/cctl.htm
Target Audience. Community college faculty and supervisory personnel
Program Description. A professional development sequence is designed
to increase teaching effectiveness of faculty and to build the instructional
leadership of supervisory personnel. It leads to a certificate of professional
development with completion of the first four courses and a master's of edu-
cation (Ed.M.) after the completion of all eight courses.

Institute for Community College Development at Cornell
    Cornell University
    411 Kennedy Hall
    Ithaca, NY 14853
    Phone: (607) 255–8236
    E-mail: iccd-mailbox@cornell.edu
    Web site: http://www.iccd.cornell.edu
Target Audience. Community colleges, administrators, and faculty
Program Description. This partnership between Cornell University and
the State University of New York offers professional development in on-site
workshops in topics such as conflict management, interest-based negotiation, and performance management.

Mid-Career Fellowship Program at Princeton University
    Theodore K. Rabb
    Mid-Career Fellowship Program
    Department of History
    Princeton, NJ 08544–1017
    Phone: (609) 258–4994
    E-mail: tkr@princeton.edu
    Web site: http://www.princeton.edu/~mcfp
Target Audience. Community college leaders and faculty from the
eleven colleges participating in the Princeton University Community
College Partnership
Program Description. This partnership between Princeton and the New
Jersey community colleges allows participants to take one course in their
own discipline at Princeton and to attend a special yearlong seminar linking faculty with administrators in exploring issues facing community colleges.
    Costs. All tuition costs are waived for fellows. Fellows are responsible
for travel expenses and course materials.

Degree Programs Offered by Universities

The following selections represent graduate programs offered by universities that have a focus on community college leadership and provide opportunities to pursue master's and doctoral degrees.

Colorado State University
   Community College Leadership Program
   College of Applied Human Sciences
   School of Education
   233 Education Building
   Fort Collins, CO 80523
   Phone: (970) 491–5199
   Web site: http://www.colostate.edu/Depts/CCLeader
   Target Audience. Individuals with master's degrees who are preparing
for instructional leadership or administrative leadership in the community
colleges
   Program Description. Student cohorts provide the context for developing leadership and team-building skills while supporting completion of a
doctoral program.

Oregon State University Community College Leadership Program
   George Copa
   Phone: (541) 737–8201
   E-mail: copag@oregonstate.edu
   Web site: http://oregonstate.edu/education/programs/cclp.html
   Target Audience. Community college teachers and administrators with
at least three years of professional experience relating to teaching, learning,
or leadership
   Program Description. Program focus is on the application of current
research to problems in education as they pertain to community colleges.
Classes are scheduled for an intensive weekend once a month at an off-
campus conference center in Oregon. This program offers the Ed.D. degree
with a concentration in community colleges.

University of California-Los Angeles (UCLA) Graduate School of Education
and Information Studies
   Office of Student Services
   University of California-Los Angeles
   1009 Moore Hall
   Los Angeles, CA 90095
   Phone: (310) 825–8326
   E-mail: info@gseis.ucla.edu
   Web site: http://www.gseis.ucla.edu

Program Description. Two of UCLA's degree programs in the Graduate School of Education and Information Studies serve those interested in community colleges. The Educational Leadership Program offers an Ed.D. degree for community college administrators. The Higher Education and Organizational Change division offers M.A. and Ph.D. degrees for students interested in research on community colleges.

University of South Florida Department of Leadership Development
   Jan Ignash
   College of Education
   Department of Leadership Development
   Tampa, FL 33620
   Phone: (813) 974–3420
   E-mail: ignash@tempest.coedu.usf.edu
   Web site: http://www.coedu.usf.edu/ache/highered.htm
   Program Description. Offers Ph.D. programs in higher education administration and in higher education curriculum and instruction with an emphasis in college teaching. It also offers an Ed.D. program in educational leadership with a community college emphasis, an M.A. in junior college teaching, and a graduate certificate in college teaching.

University of Southern California Rossier School of Education
   Linda Serra Hagedorn
   Associate Professor, Program Chair
   Community College Leadership
   Waite Phillips Hall, 500B
   Los Angeles, CA 90089–0031
   Web site: www.usc.edu/dept/education/eddcon.html
   Program Description. This program enrolls working professionals interested in careers in administration at two-year colleges and four-year colleges and universities. Offers a community college leadership certificate and an Ed.D. degree with a specialty in educational leadership focused on either two- or four-year institutions.

University of Texas at Austin Community College Leadership Program
   University of Texas at Austin
   One University Station, D5600
   Austin, TX 78712–0378
   Phone: (512) 471–7545; fax: (512) 471–9426
   Web site: http://www.utexas.edu/academic/cclp/
   Program Description. The Community College Leadership Program offers Ed.D. and Ph.D. degrees in community college leadership. Course work is supplemented by field placement in internships. More than 550 students have graduated from the program since its inception in 1944.

Additional Resources

Anderson, J. A. "Leadership Training Initiatives for Community College Administrators: A Focused Synthesis of the Literature." *Community College Review*, 1997, 24(4), 27–54.

Baynum, T. B. *An Analysis of the Content of Community College Leadership Programs in the United States: A Delphi Study.* Waco, Tex.: Baylor University, 2000.

Bragg, D. "Doing Their Best: Exemplary Graduate Leadership Programs." *Community College Journal,* Aug./Sept. 2002, 73(1), 49–53.

Cook, S. L. *An Evaluation of the University of Kentucky Community College Leadership Academy: The First Five Years.* Lexington: University of Kentucky, 2000.

Ebbers, L. H., Gallisath, G., Rockel, V., and Coyan, M. N. "The Leadership Institute for a New Century: LINCing Women and Minorities into Tomorrow's Community College Leadership Roles." *Community College Journal of Research and Practice,* 2000, 24, 375–382.

Gorham, L. S. *The North Carolina Community College Leadership Program: Impact on Career Achievement as Perceived by Women Participants.* Raleigh: North Carolina State University, 2000.

Laden, B. V. "The Role of Professional Associations in Developing Academic and Administrative Leaders." *New Directions for Community Colleges* no. 24. San Francisco: Jossey-Bass, 1996, pp. 47–58.

Villadsen, A. "Collective Wisdom, Clones, and New Creations." *Community College Journal,* Aug./Sept. 2002, 73(1), 38–41.

KAREN A. KIM *is a doctoral student in higher education and organizational change at University of California, Los Angeles.*

INDEX

Back Issue/Subscription Order Form

Copy or detach and send to:
Jossey-Bass, A Wiley Company, 989 Market Street, San Francisco CA 94103-1741

Call or fax toll-free: Phone 888-378-2537 6:30AM – 3PM PST; Fax 888-481-2665

Back Issues: Please send me the following issues at $28 each
(Important: please include ISBN number with your order.)

_____

_____

_____

$ _____   Total for single issues

$ _____   SHIPPING CHARGES: SURFACE   Domestic Canadian

	First Item	$5.00	$6.00
	Each Add'l Item	$3.00	$1.50

For next-day and second-day delivery rates, call the number listed above.

Subscriptions   Please __ start __ renew my subscription to *New Directions for Community Colleges* for the year 2____at the following rate:

U.S.	__ Individual $70	__ Institutional $149
Canada	__ Individual $70	__ Institutional $189
All Others	__ Individual $94	__ Institutional $223
Online Subscription		__ Institutional $149

**For more information about online subscriptions visit
www.interscience.wiley.com**

$ _____   Total single issues and subscriptions (Add appropriate sales tax for your state for single issue orders. No sales tax for U.S. subscriptions. Canadian residents, add GST for subscriptions and single issues.)

__Payment enclosed (U.S. check or money order only)
__VISA __ MC __ AmEx __ # _____Exp. Date _____

Signature _____ Day Phone _____
__ Bill Me (U.S. institutional orders only. Purchase order required.)

Purchase order # _____
              Federal Tax ID13559302   **GST 89102 8052**

Name _____

Address _____

_____

Phone _____ E-mail _____

For more information about Jossey-Bass, visit our Web site at **www.josseybass.com**

PROMOTION CODE ND03

**NEW DIRECTIONS FOR COMMUNITY COLLEGES
IS NOW AVAILABLE ONLINE AT WILEY INTERSCIENCE**

What is Wiley InterScience?

Wiley InterScience is the dynamic online content service from John Wiley &
Sons delivering the full text of over 300 leading scientific, technical, medical,
and professional journals, plus major reference works, the acclaimed *Current
Protocols* laboratory manuals, and even the full text of select Wiley print books
online.

What are some special features of Wiley InterScience?

Wiley InterScience Alerts is a service that delivers table of contents via e-mail
for any journal available on Wiley InterScience as soon as a new issue is
published online.
Early View is Wiley's exclusive service presenting individual articles online as
soon as they are ready, even before the release of the compiled print issue.
These articles are complete, peer-reviewed, and citable.
CrossRef is the innovative multi-publisher reference linking system enabling
readers to move seamlessly from a reference in a journal article to the cited
publication, typically located on a different server and published by a different
publisher.

How can I access Wiley InterScience?

Visit http://www.interscience.wiley.com

Guest Users can browse Wiley InterScience for unrestricted access to journal
Tables of Contents and Article Abstracts, or use the powerful search engine.
Registered Users are provided with a *Personal Home Page* to store and
manage customized alerts, searches, and links to favorite journals and articles.
Additionally, Registered Users can view free Online Sample Issues and preview
selected material from major reference works.
Licensed Customers are entitled to access full-text journal articles in PDF, with
select journals also offering full-text HTML.

How do I become an Authorized User?

Authorized Users are individuals authorized by a paying Customer to have
access to the journals in Wiley InterScience. For example, a university that
subscribes to Wiley journals is considered to be the Customer. Faculty, staff and
students authorized by the university to have access to those journals in Wiley
InterScience are Authorized Users. Users should contact their Library for information on which Wiley journals they have access to in Wiley InterScience.

ASK YOUR INSTITUTION ABOUT WILEY INTERSCIENCE TODAY!